CHILDREN'S SPIRITUALITY IN EARLY CHILDHOOD EDUCATION

This pioneering volume provides a thorough understanding of children's spirituality from a holistic development perspective and explores the ways early childhood educators can nurture spirituality in the secular classroom. Making a critical distinction between spirituality and religion, this book draws on conceptual and empirical research, as well as authentic classroom vignettes to explore how theory translates into practice. Inviting readers to examine how their beliefs inform their practices, *Children's Spirituality in Early Childhood Education* offers a purposeful window into supporting children's learning and development with a focus on their souls, making it important reading for teachers, teacher candidates, researchers, and teacher educators in the field of early childhood education.

Jennifer Mata-McMahon is Associate Professor of Early Childhood Education and Director of the Sherman Center for Early Learning in Urban Communities at the University of Maryland, Baltimore County, USA.

Patricia Escarfuller holds a certification as an AMI Montessori Elementary Teacher and as a K-12 Art Teacher. She currently teaches second-grade Social Studies and Science in Spanish and in English at Lakeland Elementary Middle School, USA.

CHILDREN'S SPIRITUALITY IN EARLY CHILDHOOD EDUCATION

Theory to Practice

Jennifer Mata-McMahon and Patricia Escarfuller

NEW YORK AND LONDON

Designed cover image: MEG

First published 2024
by Routledge
605 Third Avenue, New York, NY 10158

and by Routledge
4 Park Square, Milton Park, Abingdon, Oxon, OX14 4RN

Routledge is an imprint of the Taylor & Francis Group, an informa business

© 2024 Jennifer Mata-McMahon and Patricia Escarfuller

The right of Jennifer Mata-McMahon and Patricia Escarfuller to be
identified as authors of this work has been asserted in accordance with
sections 77 and 78 of the Copyright, Designs and Patents Act 1988.

All rights reserved. No part of this book may be reprinted or reproduced
or utilised in any form or by any electronic, mechanical, or other means,
now known or hereafter invented, including photocopying and recording,
or in any information storage or retrieval system, without permission in
writing from the publishers.

Trademark notice: Product or corporate names may be trademarks or
registered trademarks, and are used only for identification and explanation
without intent to infringe.

Library of Congress Cataloging-in-Publication Data
Names: Mata-McMahon, Jennifer, author. | Escarfuller, Patricia, author.
Title: Children's spirituality in early childhood education : theory to
    practice / Jennifer Mata-McMahon, Patricia Escarfuller.
Identifiers: LCCN 2022061868 | ISBN 9780367533380 (hardback) |
    ISBN 9780367533335 (paperback) | ISBN 9781003081463 (ebook)
Subjects: LCSH: Early childhood education—Religious aspects. |
    Spirituality—Study and teaching.
Classification: LCC LB1139.23 .M375 2023 | DDC 372.21—dc23/
    eng/20230223
LC record available at https://lccn.loc.gov/2022061868

ISBN: 978-0-367-53338-0 (hbk)
ISBN: 978-0-367-53333-5 (pbk)
ISBN: 978-1-003-08146-3 (ebk)

DOI: 10.4324/9781003081463

Typeset in Bembo
by Apex CoVantage, LLC

CONTENTS

List of Figures	*viii*
Acknowledgments	*x*
Foreword	*xiii*
Preface	*xv*
Introduction	1

SECTION I
What Is Children's Spirituality?   **5**

1   Defining Spirituality and Differentiating It From Religion   7

Differentiating Spirituality From Religiosity 10
Defining Spirituality 12
    Spirituality as a Holistic View of Development 16
    Spirituality as an Innate Human Potential or Ability to
        Be Present 17
    Spirituality as the Ability to Connect and Relate
        (to Self, Others, and Other) 20
    Spirituality to Rediscover Life's Meaning and Purpose 21

2   Understanding Children's Spirituality in the Literature
    and Research   28

Studies on Children's Spiritual Meaning-Making and
    Relationships (Including to/with God) 29

vi Contents

Studies on Children's Spirituality in Education /
    Educational Settings 33
Studies on Children's Identity Formation and Sense of Self
    Through Spirituality 36

SECTION II
Spirituality in the Classroom – What Do the Teachers Say?

45

3   Looking Into Early Childhood Teachers' Perceptions of
Nurturing Spirituality   47

Research on Educators' Perception on Spirituality 49

4   How Ms. Escarfuller's Spirituality Informs Her Pedagogy   64

Defining Spirituality 64
How Spirituality Informs Pedagogy 69
   Perfection 69
   Purpose 74
   It's All in Our Favor 74
   We Are Spiritual Beings, Energy, and Manifesters 76
   Full, Complete, and Equal 78
   Needs, Mattering, and Growth 79
Montessori Human Tendencies and Pedagogy 81

5   Vignettes From Ms. Escarfuller's Classroom   88

Choice: The Material Serves the Child 88
Hands at Work 91
Movement Revealing 91
Gregariousness & Conversation 93
Time & Pacing 95
Openness & Acceptance 96
Preparation as an Adult 100
Listening for That Inner Voice 101
Gratitude 102
Finding Meaning – A Montessori Great Lesson: The Story of
   The Coming of the Universe 103

Contents **vii**

Emotional Awareness 108
Connection With Others: Friendship 112
Inner Peace 116
Connection With Nature: Our Environment 117

SECTION III
Tying It All Together   123

6   How Can We Nurture Children's Spirituality in Secular Settings?   125

Understanding Our Constitutional Constraints 126
Importance of a Holistic View of the Child and Inclusion of
  Spirituality in the Curriculum 128
Nurturing Spirituality in the Classroom – The Role of
  the Teacher 130
What Are Teachers Doing in the Classroom From a Secular
  Spirituality Perspective? 136

7   Spirituality as the North Star for Early Childhood
    Education: Where Do We Go From Here?   142

Supporting Children's Spirituality Starting in Higher
  Education 143
What Do We Need to Do? Where Do We Start? 144
Making Spirituality the North Star for Education 151

Index   *155*

FIGURES

1.1	Religion vs. spirituality	12
1.2	Definition of spirituality by categories	15
3.1	Spirituality as community (Vicky, September 11, 2019)	53
3.2	Spirituality as happiness and positivity (Ginger, September 11, 2019)	54
3.3	Spirituality as all of us and more (Megan, September 11, 2019)	55
3.4	Spirituality as bigger than ourselves (Mindy, September 11, 2019)	56
3.5	Spirituality as related to nature (Kelly, September 19, 2020)	57
3.6	Spirituality in the body (Tammy, September 19, 2020)	58
5.1	Child Geometric Cabinet work	89
5.2	Child repeating work	89
5.3	Child engaged in washing	90
5.4	Child hand sews his first pillow	92
5.5	Peace area	93
5.6	Classroom Contract	95
5.7	Talking piece and bell	98
5.8	Peace rose	99
5.9	Grace and courtesy lesson	100
5.10	God as Protector, from Evil	104
5.11	God as Protector, with Hug	105
5.12	God Creator Among Us	106
5.13	God Creator Above Us	106
5.14	God as Nature	107
5.15	God as Judge	108
5.16	God as Provider	108

Figures **ix**

5.17	God on the Cross	109
5.18	Emotion wheel	119
5.19	Tulip Project work	120
7.1	Spirituality the North Star	152

ACKNOWLEDGMENTS

When I first got the idea for this book, I thought it would be a capstone to all the work I have completed in the field of children's spirituality: the work with children (Mata, 2015), the work with pre-service teachers (Mata, 2012, 2013), the work with in-service teachers (Mata-McMahon et al., 2018, 2020), and most recently, the design and validation of the *Early Childhood Educators' Spiritual Practices in the Classroom (ECE-SPC)* instrument (Mata-McMahon et al., under review) to measure what teachers are currently doing to support children's spirituality across the U.S. These remain as some of the main components of this book. Yet, in talking to my editor at Routledge and working closely with teachers from partner schools, the idea of collaborating with a teacher embracing a pedagogy informed by a spiritual framework came to light. At first, I thought finding such an educator would be a monumental task, like searching for a mythical creature, akin to a child's desire to find a unicorn. Little did I know, magic was in the works and serendipitously, while facilitating a teacher professional development workshop, I met Ms. Escarfuller.

Patricia Escarfuller is a one-of-a-kind early childhood educator, an AMI Montessori Elementary Diploma guide, who has been able to continue, with the support of her traditional public school principal, to approach her labor of teaching young children with a guiding spiritual thread. Aside from her AMI Montessori training, Patricia has a special way of teaching and interacting with children that seems idiosyncratically unique. You will find throughout the anecdotes shared and the chapters she wrote that her voice, her mannerisms, and her intentional use of words all come together to reveal a teacher like no other. I want to thank Patricia not only for embarking with me in the arduous labor of birthing this book but also for the numerous thought-provoking meetings and conversations we had over the past years that reignited my passion for this topic and materialized through her actions in the classroom what I always dreamt for children, and she made possible. Patricia claims this was a two-way journey of nourishment for professional growth framed by the topic we embraced: spirituality. She says our relationship was akin to that of teacher and student, in which I was the teacher, and she was the pupil, who developed into the teacher she now is and shares with you in Chapters 4 and 5. I believe magic was at play, and Spirit brought us together nurturing our souls in order to actualize our purpose in this moment of our lives as this book we now share with you.

When we embarked on the task of writing this book, I was fortunate to have the possibility to work with a graduate student as a research assistant, Shahin Hossain. He is currently a doctoral student in the Department of Language, Literacy, and Culture at the University of Maryland, Baltimore County (UMBC), who contributed to this work by observing Patricia's classroom while she taught and collected some of the anecdotes shared in the subsequent chapters. He also diligently helped with updating some of the literature and held discussion sessions with both Patricia and me to learn about children's spirituality and helped each of us process what we were working on both theoretically and in practice. We thank Shahin profusely for his dedication to this project and welcome him into the field as a rising scholar.

We would also like to acknowledge Sravanti Vitta Sanjay, a graduate assistant from the Sherman Center for Early Learning in Urban Communities at UMBC, who illustrated Figure 1.1 presented in Chapter 1. As well as my talented aunt and godmother María Elena Gómez, who goes by MEG, who designed and illustrated our beautiful book cover, and Figure 7.1, the closing image for the book in Chapter 7.

We are forever thankful to our students. Thankful to my undergraduate and graduate pre-service teacher educators, who embraced with open arms the topic of spirituality in the redesigned Early Childhood Education Seminar, offering themselves with vulnerability to learn how to nurture children's spirit in secular settings. Thankful to Patricia's students, children as young as three ranging up to ten years of age, who showed up every day eager to learn and rose to the challenge of trusting her with their spirit. What we present to you in this book is a gift from them.

Lastly, but sure with no less gratitude, we thank our marvelous editors Michael A. McMahon, Dr. John L. Hochheimer, Patricia's son Kwabe A. Osei, Robert Breyer, Adriana Medina, Mary Ann Constantinides, Sidney Bridges, Dr. Margo Veal, and Rhonda Lucas-Sabater, for their insightful feedback and thought-provoking comments that have made this book even better than we ever imagined it could be.

xii Acknowledgments

References

Mata, J. (2012). Nurturing spirituality in early childhood classrooms: The teacher's view. In M. Fowler, J. D. Martin, & J. L. Hochheimer (Eds.), *Spirituality: Theory, praxis and pedagogy* (pp. 239–248). Inter-Disciplinary Press.

Mata, J. (2013). Meditation: Using it in the classroom. In W. Van Moer, D. A. Celik, & J. L. Hochheimer (Eds.), *Spirituality in the 21st century: Journeys beyond entrenched boundaries* (pp. 109–119). Inter-Disciplinary Press.

Mata, J. (2015). *Spiritual experiences in early childhood education: Four kindergarteners, one classroom.* Routledge.

Mata-McMahon, J., Haslip, M. J., & Kruse, L. (under review). Validation study of the Early Childhood Educators' Spiritual Practices in the Classroom (ECE-SPC) instrument using Rasch. *International Journal of Children's Spirituality.*

Mata-McMahon, J., Haslip, M. J., & Schein, D. L. (2018). Early childhood educators' perceptions of nurturing spirituality in secular settings. *Early Child Development and Care, 189*(14), 2233–2251. https://doi.org/10.1080/03004430.2018.1445734

Mata-McMahon, J., Haslip, M. J., & Schein, D. L. (2020). Connections, virtues, and meaning-making: How early childhood educators describe children's spirituality. *Early Childhood Education Journal, 48*(5), 657–669. https://doi.org/https://doi.org/10.1007/s10643-020-01026-8

FOREWORD

Albert Einstein is attributed to have posed, "Concerning matter, we have been all wrong. What we have called matter is energy, whose vibration has been so lowered as to be perceptible to the senses. Matter is spirit reduced to the point of visibility. There is no matter." The existence of a force within which all life exists – variously called *shakti, Ein Sof, bios, aether, Qi, Prana, Élan Vital,* or *the Life Force* – has been perceived, studied, debated, and taught for roughly 100 millennia. Human comprehension of this force has always been bounded by the limits of our senses. While some people can perceive this energy more acutely, more deeply than others, it is nonetheless true that none of us – as individuals or as groups – have ever been able, nor will we be able to comprehend it fully, limited as we are by the confines of our senses and our imaginations.

Its human comprehension, study, and explanation have been the interior soil within which the spiritual seeds of life's meanings have sprouted, germinated, grown, and spread from generation to generation, within the limits of both our senses and our beliefs in the range of human possibility. This is a source of great power. Its cultivation, broadcasting, and harvest, too, are the locus of great power as well.

As long as people have sought to comprehend this force, there have also been efforts to explain it within a unified story. *The Tanach, The New Testament, The Quran, The Upanishads, The Tao Te Ching,* and *The Avesta* are all examples (among many others) of efforts to explain the comprehension of the Life Force within a unified system of belief. In this sense, then, spiritual comprehension and understanding are the Life Force reduced, following Einstein, to the point of visibility, with each approach constituting a refracting lens through which people can examine this *Force* within their own lived experiences.

And, as long as there have been efforts to construct a unified system of belief, there have been efforts to inculcate, or to impose, that system onto others, most

xiv Foreword

especially the young (typically within the confines of a religious institution: church, synagogue, madrassa, etc.). Religious education comprises a comprehensive effort to teach children in what to believe, and how to live, think, and act consonant with a unified system of belief created by others.

This was difficult enough, millennia or centuries, or decades ago, when exposure to life outside a confined area, and ideas beyond those sanctioned by a reigning socio-political-religious system were highly limited. In our own time, however, with ubiquitous mass and digital means of communication and ease of travel, exposure to competing belief systems (and, therefore, divergent claims to truth) is almost a given in most of the world. As many of us in the modern age have seen, it becomes ever-easier and increasingly simple to become overwhelmed by competing external claims of truth.

This is when the importance of a more broadly based spiritual education, with its focus on internally based contemplation and study, becomes paramount. For the past 30+ years practitioners in an ever-widening array of fields have been studying and implementing spiritual practices in their fields of work: Medicine, Nursing, Art, Dance, Music, Policing, Social Work, Community Organizing, Architecture, Business, International Relations, Anthropology, Alcohol and Drug Rehabilitation, Ecology, Education, Home Economics, Hospice and Palliative Care, Management and Leadership Studies, Perinatal Studies, Prison Rehabilitation, and more.

And, for the past 30+ years, teachers, scholars, and community workers have been developing models and practices of spiritual, as opposed to religious, education. With the more spiritually based approaches to the educational needs of children being developed so, too, must there be spiritually based approaches to the educational needs of their teachers.

That is why this book is so timely and important. Working from a holistic view of development, here will be found the rationale for why spiritual (as opposed to religious) education supports the inner lives of the young in our current age of competing claims to truth in an effort to rediscover life's meaning and purpose based on an innate Human Potential or Ability to be Present to one's self, to others, and to the Other (however that manifests in the individual's lived experiences). Here, too, teachers will find field reports on differing approaches to spiritually centered education in non-sectarian schools citing practices that have been found to be particularly effective.

For, to paraphrase Galileo Galilei, "We cannot teach a man [children] anything; we can only help him [them] find it within themselves" (Tillman, 2021).

John L. Hochheimer, Ph.D., Professor Emeritus
Southern Illinois University Carbondale
December 2022

Reference

Tillman, N. T. (2021). *Galileo Galilei: Biography, inventions & other facts.* Galileo Quotes, n.p. Retrieved December 22, 2022, from www.space.com/15589-galileo-galilei.html

PREFACE

The concept behind this volume derives from my own experience as a child in search of answers to life's big, typically unanswerable questions. It comes from a desire to support adults in children's lives, to provide the framework for these questions to be explored, and for meaning to be discovered for those asking these questions. Because I am an early childhood educator by training, and a teacher educator by trade, I feel compelled to share the knowledge and experience I have gathered over two decades of working with children and researching in the field of children's spirituality.

The main goal is to support early childhood educators in understanding children's spirituality from a secular perspective, making the case for it being a topic that can be supported and nurtured in public settings, as it is a different construct from religion, religiosity, or even religious practices. To achieve this goal, I have paired with a colleague and friend, Patricia Escarfuller, who has been working with children as a traditionally certified teacher since 1997 and as an AMI Montessori diplomaed teacher since 2019. The book thus compiles years of conceptual and empirical work I have conducted as a researcher and scholar in the field of children's spirituality, as well as the views of a currently practicing early childhood educator working with bilingual children, using a Montessori framework in supporting spirituality for her students, while teaching them core-curricular content areas and following state and national mandated standards for teaching and learning.

It is our hope that this volume will inspire other early childhood educators in opening their classroom doors to spirituality, in search of supporting a holistic type of education for their students, including the spiritual essence of the child, as well as all other areas of development to inform their pedagogical and curricular decisions.

INTRODUCTION

Since the turn of the new century, and more specifically immediately after the September 11, 2001, attack on the U.S., acts of violence centered around misbeliefs in the name of religion or religious practices have seemed to become more prevalent. We could explain these acts as coming from outside our country's borders, and thus not take responsibility for them. Yet more recently, we have been experiencing the devastating consequences of hatred coming from the inside; our own people are turning against each other, and the acts of violence can no longer be dismissed as the responsibility of others.

When identifying the main social institution responsible for developing citizens to live in a democratic society, in which we all contribute to living in peace and if not embracing it, at least respecting differences among us, and accepting and including all individuals, we would immediately think of Education. Traditionally, education has been responsible for preparing and teaching citizens to participate in society, without conforming to it, but contributing to its change and progress. I pose that for children to become these citizens we so desperately need, spirituality needs to be re-embraced in schools. Education can be, as it once was, the ultimate place to provide guidance regarding moral and ethical values to students, if we include spiritual nourishment and prioritize it in our curricula. In this book, I explained how this can be done.

My interest in spirituality stems from the urgent need to nurture the whole child, and not only give prevalence to children's cognitive and language development as is typically done in classrooms today. As a social-constructivist early childhood educator, holding a holistic understanding of the child, I believe that all aspects of being human are the purview of education, and thus my responsibility as an educator supersedes academics. Through my work on children's spirituality, I have come to

DOI: 10.4324/9781003081463-1

2 Introduction

define spirituality as "an innate human characteristic, a potential we are all born with, which allows us to connect with something beyond us (transcendence or divine), feel part of the greater universe, and be connected to otherness" (Mata, 2015). For me, spirituality encompasses the individual capacity and the essence of life, providing us with a window to a greater consciousness and a more profound understanding of being, meaning, and purpose. Thus, it is through spirituality that we may both discover our life's purpose and accomplish it to its full potential.

It is from this understanding of spirituality, as distinctive from religion, that I approach my work. Religion understood as a belief or acknowledgment of a superhuman power or powers (e.g., god or gods) held by a human community, typically manifested in obedience, reverence, and worship involving adherence to a codified set of beliefs and practices as part of a system defining a code of living (Oxford English Dictionary, 2023), differs greatly from my understanding of spirituality. Spirituality does not imply shared beliefs or practices; it does not need to be codified or adhered to. Spirituality is an innate potential that can be explored, expanded, and nurtured if we are called to do so. It is an individual endeavor, one that we choose to pursue if so encouraged, and I believe it is part of educators' responsibility to inspire their students to do so.

Nevertheless, spirituality in the U.S. is mostly absent from education, specifically when referring to the education imparted in public schools. Policymakers and educators tend to believe that spirituality is as similar, if not one and the same, as religion and thus banned from public educational settings. This belief is based on the separation of church and state, a concept expressed in the First Amendment to the Constitution, which states, "Congress shall make no law respecting an establishment of religion, or prohibiting the free exercise thereof" (Waggoner, 2003). In mistaking spirituality for religion, and in misunderstanding the possible limitations implied in the separation of church and state, teachers tend to believe that spirituality should not be, and ultimately is not, nurtured within public schools. However, Carpenter (2003) explains, "we should remember that not only do the courts forbid any action by government schools not prompted by a 'secular primary purpose' or which would 'principally and primarily' aid religion; they also forbid any that would inhibit it" (p. 44). Therefore, making sure proselytizing does not occur in classrooms does not in turn prompt teachers to ignore or, even worse, to repress children's spiritual beliefs and their nourishment. Ignoring, preventing, or discounting spirituality and spiritual talk, experiences, and expressions is a way of restraining them, ultimately negating the children their right to have their spiritual selves acknowledged, nurtured, and not inhibited.

Conversely, in my work with in-service teachers, I found that early childhood educators deem spirituality important, they understand its value, and even believe that there is a space in the classroom for it, yet convey their lack of preparedness to facilitate this for the children they serve (Mata, 2012). They share that neither their teacher preparation programs nor their professional development experiences have prepared them to address spirituality in the classroom. In fact, most teachers I have spoken with about this topic share that they had never discussed spirituality in the context of education before our encounter and would very much want to know how to promote, support, and nurture spirituality for the children under their care.

It is with this need in mind that I wish to write a book that sets the focus on children's spirituality as the main component missing from early childhood education, that should be not only included but taken as the guiding North Star that propels how we teach and nurture children. Kessler (2000) explains, "many classrooms are spiritually empty, not by accident, but by design" (p. xii). I propose to make the case for embracing spirituality by reviewing the research advanced in this field, the work completed with pre-service and in-service early childhood educators who understand the importance of nurturing the whole child, and by offering resources highlighting what is currently happening in classrooms across the U.S. and how this knowledge can be used for nurturing the spirit of the child and incorporating spirituality into the classroom.

This book will serve as a capstone compilation of the work I have embarked on for the past decades, establishing connections between children's spirituality and the field of early childhood education (Mata, 2011, 2015; Mata-McMahon, 2018a, 2019). As well as a launching point to a proposition for a major redesign of our educational system, one that would return the child to the center stage, asking teachers to adjust their focus and to center their practice around the child's spirit, alongside their mind and body. As an early childhood educator, my interest in children and their optimal development is at the heart of what guides my work; this coupled with my ever-growing interest in spirituality found a natural marriage as I advanced my work as a scholar and researcher. As a teacher educator, it seems only natural that I see the solution to our systemic social issues through education and specifically possible through teacher preparation programs.

This volume contains:

(1) a review of the scholarship that has informed my theoretical and conceptual framework and my ever-developing definition of spirituality (Mata, 2015; Mata-McMahon, 2018b, 2019); and a review of the research conducted with children in order to better understand what children's spirituality entails and how to nurture it in the classroom (Mata-McMahon, 2016);

(2) what I have found to be pre-service and in-service early childhood educators' understandings of spirituality and perceptions of nurturing spirituality in the classroom (Mata, 2012, 2014; Mata-McMahon et al., 2020), particularly highlighting the experiences in Ms. Escarfuller's classrooms, which will be shared by her, informed by her training in the Montessori philosophy; and

(3) what is being done currently in early childhood classrooms across the U.S. (Mata-McMahon et al., 2018) and how teachers can intentionally nurture children's spirituality in secular, public educational settings, as well as what the future holds for early childhood education and what can be done specifically in teacher preparation programs.

4 Introduction

A few resources to be used in the classroom such as books, materials, and curriculum guides are mentioned throughout the text but are not the focus of this volume. These will be incorporated and further developed in a future volume consisting of a resource book to be used by early childhood practitioners who wish to nurture spirituality in their educational settings.

References

Carpenter, W. A. (2003). Jacob's children and ours: Richard of St. Victor's curriculum of the soul. *Educational Horizons, 82*(1), 44–54.

Kessler, R. (2000). *The soul of education: Helping students find connection, compassion, and character at school.* Association for Supervision and Curriculum Development.

Mata, J. (2011). *Children's spirituality as experienced and expressed in a kindergarten classroom* [Dissertation, Teachers College, Columbia University]. ProQuest, UMI Dissertation Publishing.

Mata, J. (2012). Nurturing spirituality in early childhood classrooms: The teacher's view. In M. Fowler, J. D. Martin, & J. L. Hochheimer (Eds.), *Spirituality: Theory, praxis and pedagogy* (pp. 239–248). Inter-Disciplinary Press.

Mata, J. (2014). Sharing my journey and opening spaces: Spirituality in the classroom. *International Journal of Children's Spirituality, 19*(2), 112–122. https://doi.org/10.1080/1364436X.2014.922464

Mata, J. (2015). *Spiritual experiences in early childhood education: Four kindergarteners, one classroom.* Routledge.

Mata-McMahon, J. (2016). Reviewing the research in children's spirituality (2005–2015): Proposing a pluricultural approach. *International Journal of Children's Spirituality, 21*(2), 140–152. https://doi.org/10.1080/1364436X.2016.1186611

Mata-McMahon, J. (2018a). Early childhood educators nurturing children's spirituality: Making connections with play. In D. Schein (Ed.), *Play, policy, & practice connections.* NAEYC.

Mata-McMahon, J. (2018b). What do kindergarteners' spiritual experiences and expressions look like in a secular classroom? In B. Espinoza, J. R. Estep, & S. Morgenthaler (Eds.), *Story, formation, and culture: From theory to practice in ministry with children* (pp. 235–252). Pickwick Publications.

Mata-McMahon, J. (2019). Exploring connections between humor and children's spirituality. In E. Loizou & S. Recchia (Eds.), *Research on young children's humor: Theoretical and practical implications for early childhood education* (pp. 223–241). Springer.

Mata-McMahon, J., Haslip, M. J., & Schein, D. L. (2018). Early childhood educators' perceptions of nurturing spirituality in secular settings. *Early Child Development and Care, 189*(14), 2233–2251. https://doi.org/10.1080/03004430.2018.1445734

Mata-McMahon, J., Haslip, M. J., & Schein, D. L. (2020). Connections, virtues, and meaning-making: How early childhood educators describe children's spirituality. *Early Childhood Education Journal, 48*(5), 657–669. https://doi.org/10.1007/s10643-020-01026-8

Oxford English Dictionary. (2023). Religion, *n.* In *Oxford English Dictionary.* https://www.oed.com/viewdictionaryentry/Entry/161944

Waggoner, M. D. (2003). Reading the terrain: Environmental factors influencing religious literacy initiatives in educator preparation. *Educational Horizons, 82*(1), 74–84.

SECTION I

What Is Children's Spirituality?

This section sets the stage for making the case for the importance of nurturing spirituality for children. It begins with Chapter 1, by defining spirituality and differentiating it from religion, highlighting the opportunity that teachers are afforded to take on the responsibility to nurture spirituality in the classroom, even when this responsibility is undertaken in public schools. Following, in Chapter 2, the literature is reviewed to explore how spirituality has been defined and thus utilized in research pertaining to early childhood, specifically in educational settings.

DOI: 10.4324/9781003081463-2

1

DEFINING SPIRITUALITY AND DIFFERENTIATING IT FROM RELIGION

Spirituality tends to be ubiquitous, yet unsurprisingly it is difficult to define; the ineffability of this concept is due to its ethereal nature. Coupled with this is the fact that spirituality tends to be lived and expressed in very personal, individual manners; thus, arriving at a consensus on its definition is quite challenging. Nevertheless, I will try to forecast what scholars and researchers have contributed to our collective understanding of spirituality and how we come to define it, as well as to put forth my own definition of spirituality, one that I use to ground the work I advance in the field of children's spirituality. In Chapter 4, Patricia will share her definition of spirituality and how it plays out in her classroom, underpinning the pedagogical strategies she designs for her students.

Spirituality, as a concept, is often used indistinctively from religion, religiosity, and religiousness. Nonetheless, there are significant differences between these two constructs. Religion can be understood and thus defined as a unified system of dogmatic practices and shared beliefs related to the sacred, which unite all who adhere to them into a single community (Durkheim, 1915). These beliefs guide individuals' actions and provide a structure for their worldview. Religions have existed since antiquity. In their search to discover their origins, humans have revered deities and creators since the beginning of time, coming together as collectives to proclaim faith in certain beliefs and values, giving way to religion.

Religious practices have been part of civilization since prehistoric times. In 120,000 BC, during the Stone Age, the "Neanderthal graves and feasting rituals are the first evidence of human religious activity" (Smith, 2007, p. 4). Wunn (2000) explains, regardless of controversial debates among archaeologists, there seems to be

DOI: 10.4324/9781003081463-3

8 What Is Children's Spirituality?

an accepted fact in the field of History of Religion that Paleolithic man (*sic*) had a (*sic*) specific religion (*sic*). They performed rituals related to hunting and believed in a master of animals. They buried the dead and acknowledged a life after death.

(p. 419)

Organized religion as we know it today was evidenced for the first time around the middle of the fourth millennium B.C. along with the transition from village culture to urban settlements and the first cities, such as Lagash, Ur, and Nippur . . . regarded as the first literate societies, the civilizations of Mesopotamia.

(Smith, 2007, p. 10)

Historically, spirituality was not distinguished from religiousness until the rise of secularism in the twentieth century, resulting from a popular disillusionment with religious institutions perceived as a limitation to personal experiences of the sacred (Turner et al., 1995). In pursuit of establishing the difference between religiousness and spirituality, Zinnbauer and colleagues (1999) used three major dimensions in their description of these constructs: negative-positive, organized-personal, and substantive-functional. Regarding the negative-positive dimension, they found religion is often associated with negative qualities (e.g., being dogmatic or encouraging cult and fundamentalist behavior), whereas spirituality is typically associated with positive or 'good' qualities (e.g., expanding self-awareness). The organized-personal dimension showed religion representing a set of organized practices established by tradition and conducted in a central place of worship, whereas spirituality was considered more personal, consisting of a 'lived consciousness' of relating to a higher power. Lastly, the substantial-functional dimension showed religion holding a substantive focus on its practices, beliefs, and emotions, whereas spirituality was considered more functional, focusing on nature and being, and how beliefs, emotions, and practices related to diverse life events like death, suffering, and injustice (Zinnbauer et al., 1999). "Some argue that both religion and spirituality entail theistic concepts of the sacred, such as a belief in God, Christ, or the Divine, but that spirituality also encompasses beliefs in New Age concepts such as astrology or the supernatural (Koenig, 1997)" (cited in Schlehofer et al., 2008. p. 412). Nonetheless, Zinnbauer and colleagues (1997) found within a sample of 346 individuals of varying backgrounds and religious beliefs that, when describing spirituality, 70 percent of respondents used what the researchers deemed 'traditional' concepts of the sacred, such as beliefs in God or Christ, versus 10 percent who made references to 'nontraditional' concepts, such as nature, transcendental reality, or ground of being (cited in Schlehofer et al., 2008).

Hill and colleagues (2000) proposed a different, nonpolarized conceptualization of religion and spirituality. In this conceptualization, both religion and spirituality encompass two main components: (1) a concept of the sacred (i.e., a perception of some source of ultimate reality or divine being/object) and (2) a search for what is sacred (i.e., the articulation – at least to oneself – of understanding and maintaining a relationship with one's own personal representation of divinity).

> Religion, however, encompasses two additional components that spirituality does not: (3) a search for the nonsacred (e.g., feelings of safety, hope, or affiliation arising out of a sense of community within a religious group); and (4) a prescription of legitimate means and methods by which to search for the sacred (e.g., religious rituals such as baptism, religious wedding ceremonies, and organized prayers).
>
> *(Schlehofer et al., 2008, p. 412)*

Furthermore, spirituality is often described in personal or experiential terms, such as having a relationship with a higher power (Zinnbauer et al., 1997). It may include reference to an inner guide or 'moral compass' and can exist within or independent of a religious context (Marler & Hadaway, 2002). In fact, in one of the studies reviewed, Marler and Hadaway (2002) found, "63 percent of participants saw religion and spirituality as two distinct, yet closely related, concepts, and [only] one-third reported that they found the terms to be nearly one and the same" (Schlehofer et al., 2008, p. 413).

A study conducted with 67 older adults from three different religious and non-religiously affiliated retirement communities in Los Angeles County, California, found that "older adults largely view the concepts of religion and spirituality not as polarized, but rather as distinct concepts that nonetheless share considerable overlap" (Schlehofer et al., 2008, p. 424).

Interestingly, "the findings that religion is seen as providing a guiding framework by which to live one's life and a sense of community, while spirituality does not, have implications for work with, and measurement of, these constructs" (Schlehofer et al., 2008, p. 424). These findings act as a propeller to encourage the work we present in this text. We believe spirituality does provide the framework, at a personal level, and perhaps varying from one individual to the next, for children to begin to explore their life's purpose and live a life of fulfillment in what they came to be, learn, and experience during this lifetime. Through supporting spirituality in the classroom, teachers can begin to build a community in which children feel safe to experience and express their spiritual selves, without needing to subscribe to or negate any religious framework they might be part of. Teachers can support children in revealing their true selves and, if so needed, encourage them to remember who they are and what they are here to do.

However, religion has made its way into the heart of society, immersing itself in everything humans do, including the ways we educate our children and youth. In modern society, educational settings have traditionally been the way to socialize and enculturate young minds, in the hopes to mold them into upstanding

10 What Is Children's Spirituality?

citizens of their particular social groups. It is no wonder that religion, as a man-made social construct that can be used to indoctrinate and control populations, has been inserted into education across the world. In the U.S. however, because of the constitutional separation of church and state, we typically do not find religion or religious education in public secular educational settings since these schools are often funded by state funds. Thus, it is a pervasive understanding among U.S. educators that religious content or any type of proselytization is forbidden in public, secular schools, and by extension, so is spirituality. By going deeper into the differences between religion and spirituality I hope to demystify the notion that spirituality does not belong in the classroom and show ways in which it can be nurtured. A wider explanation of the meaning of the separation of church and state will be further explained in Chapter 6 when looking at how spirituality can be nurtured in secular educational settings.

Differentiating Spirituality From Religiosity

In a survey of the current global religious landscape, Hackett et al. (2017) explain that more than 80 percent of the global population identifies as religious, and even a higher percentage identifies as spiritual. This propels a search to better comprehend what is understood as religious versus spiritual, and how these identities manifest themselves in people's daily lives, particularly in educational settings.

When religion is attempted to be understood, definitions that include the belief in and worship of a superhuman controlling power, especially a personal God or gods, are commonly found. These definitions include a particular system of faith and worship or pursuit or interest to which someone ascribes supreme importance. In my previous works, I have used different definitions, such as religion is a codified set of beliefs and practices, held true and agreed upon by a group of people. Yet, I have found the following definition as one of the most illustrative, "religion is a set of beliefs concerning the cause, nature, and purpose of the universe, (. . .) usually involving devotional and ritual observances, and often containing a moral code governing the conduct of human affairs" (Dictionary.com). Furthermore, religiosity as the practice of religion has been defined as participation in a unified system of beliefs and practices relative to sacred things (Durkheim, 1915).

On Character Clearinghouse, contributing editor Patrick Love (2000) differentiates spirituality from religiosity arguing that they are distinctively different, yet overlapping, concepts. Mainly, the overlap is that in both concepts there is a concern for that which exists beyond the corporal, rational, and visible universe, and both attempt to provide means for understanding or knowing that which lies beyond our physical, time-bound world. Some of the differences mentioned by Love stem from overlaps in which the concepts differ slightly. For example, when discussing spirituality, the term supernatural is used explicitly in the sense of that which exists beyond the natural world, whereas issues of deity and divine power

Defining Spirituality and Differentiating It From Religion   **11**

as it relates to the supernatural pertain to the concept of religion. Likely, both definitions have a focus on activity. However, religion embodies action through rituals, prayers, and exercises, whereas spirituality connotes action and movement, through process, transcending, developing, deriving, and exploring.

Lastly, a salient difference between religion and spirituality lies in how they engage with the internal and external dimensions of being. Religion tends to begin and mostly remains as an external phenomenon; its primary concern is external to the visible world, centered on the existence of a supreme being, and includes an agreed-upon set of beliefs and practices that are external to the individual. Spirituality begins with and is perpetually an internal process, even though there is movement from oneself through self-transcendence, connectedness to self and others, and relationships with that which lies beyond the known world. Van Niekerk (2018) makes the distinction clear when defining spirituality as "the opposite of materiality; that it is distinct from body; that it is different from religion; that it is distinctive from the secular epitomized in the now frequently used acronym, SBNR, which stands for: spiritual but not religious" (p. 8).

Nevertheless, there seems to be a strongly held societal assumption that religious and spiritual are synonymous (Love, 2000). Similarly, for some scholars, particularly those working in the field of religious education, practicing religion is often presented and understood interchangeably with the notion of being spiritual.

Some believe that one cannot be religious if one is not spiritual. However, I have encountered, and I am sure you have as well, individuals who are devout to their religious practices, yet are completely disconnected from the needs of their families, neighbors, other living beings, or even nature. In other words, they do not seem very spiritual, yet are undoubtedly faithful to their religious practices. I have also encountered people that claim to be agnostic or even atheist and yet are caring toward others in ways that only a deeply spiritual being would be. Yes, we can be religious and spiritual at the same time, yet we can also be spiritual and not religious at all. From these distinctions, I propose spirituality as an independent concept that can be defined in quite a different way other than the way we define religiosity. Because of this, it needs to be considered its own unique construct, separate from our understanding of religion or religiosity, and not be used interchangeably.

Figure 1.1 illustrates the difference between religion and spirituality, as I understand it. Religion is shown as a container through which spirituality can be lived as long as we stay within that provided structure. Spirituality is illustrated as the essence in which we live our lives as souls, or consciousness, in a human body. In this image the goldfish represent humans, the water represents spirituality, and the fishbowl represents religion. Note how the fishbowl is open and both fish can choose to experience spirituality from within or outside of the fishbowl, regardless the bowl will always exist, as well as the water, and the fish. Ultimately, it is up to human beings to decide how they want to experience and express spirituality.

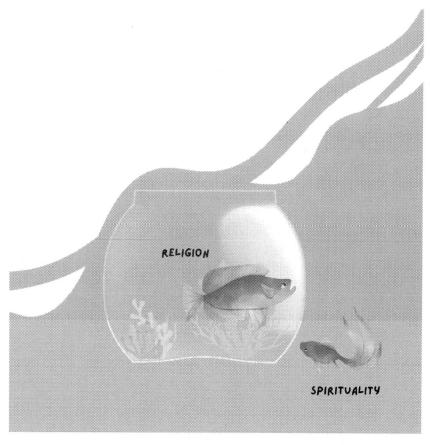

FIGURE 1.1 Religion vs. spirituality

Source: Sravanti Vitta Sanjay

Defining Spirituality

The origins of the world spirituality can be found in the Latin noun *spiritualitas* associated with the adjective *spiritualis* (spiritual), and the noun *spiritus*, meaning 'breath of life' (Elkins et al., 1988). These words ultimately derive from the Greek noun *pneuma*, spirit, and the adjective *pneumatikos* (Sheldrake, 2013). In the Middle Ages, spirituality as a noun most frequently referred to the clerical state. Looking at it from a Christian lens, Sheldrake (2013) explains, "the noun only became established in reference to 'the spiritual life' in seventeenth century France – sometimes in a pejorative sense" (p. 2). Later, it disappeared from theological circles until the nineteenth and beginning of the twentieth centuries,

Defining Spirituality and Differentiating It From Religion **13**

when it began appearing again in French writings in a positive sense as it referenced the 'spiritual life' as the heart of Christian existence. Subsequently, it could be found in English as French writings were translated. The use of the word spirituality reemerged in the twentieth century after the Second Vatican Council in the early 1960s, beginning to dominate and replace terms such as ascetical theology or mystical theology, becoming the preferred term to describe studies of Christian life from the 1970s onward (Sheldrake, 2013).

More recently, defining spirituality has proven to be difficult, since it is used in a wide range of contexts. Sheldrake (2013), for example, explains that spirituality comprises what is holistic, meaning a fully integrated approach to life, relating to the concept of the holy and attending to life as a whole. While Garcia-Romeu (2010) defines spirituality, or more so spiritual acceptance, as a stable shift in worldview toward belief in forces that cannot be rationally comprehended or objectively proven. Furthermore, spirituality is understood as engaging in a quest for the sacred, which include a broader understanding of the numinous. Concurrently, spirituality is also frequently understood to involve a quest for meaning, for purpose of life, and for a sense of life direction. As well, it is linked to a quest for ultimate values in contrast to an instrumentalized or purely materialistic approach to life.

Sheldrake (2013) further explicates that the majority of available definitions for spirituality "emphasize inner experience, introspection, a subjective journey, personal well-being, inner harmony or happiness" (p. 4). While Sagberg (2006) argues that there are two common elements in all accepted definitions of spirituality. The first is the human's ability and urge toward transcending the immediate, transcending the present time, and transcending the actual place in a search for meaning and coherence in life. The second is a moral sense of what it is to be truly human; a sense that might be expressed in religious as well as humanistic terms.

Furthermore, David Elkins and colleagues (1988), while looking to define spirituality from a humanistic-phenomenological perspective, explain that it is a multidimensional construct consisting of nine major components found in the spiritual person:

1. a belief in a transcendent dimension to life;
2. a knowing that life is deeply meaningful and there is a purpose to it;
3. having a sense of vocation or mission in life;
4. a belief that life is infused with sacredness offering experiences of awe, reverence, and wonder;
5. an appreciation of material goods without seeking ultimate satisfaction from them or using them as a substitute for frustrated spiritual needs;
6. altruism, as they can be affected by the pain and suffering of others;
7. a sense of idealism, having a vision and commitment to the betterment of the world;

14 What Is Children's Spirituality?

8. an awareness of the tragic realities of human existence such as pain, suffering, and death; and
9. a knowing that spirituality has a discernable effect on their relationships to self, other, nature, life, and whatever they consider to be the Ultimate.

In the early childhood education literature, as it relates to children's spirituality, there are many different definitions and ways of understanding this concept. It appears every scholar that writes on the topic has their distinctive take on the subject and proposes a unique or at least slightly different understanding of the concept of spirituality. In trying to come to a succinct definition of spirituality that reflects the definitions found in the literature, I constructed the definition that I have been using in my work in this field for over a decade.

In searching for definitions that explained religiosity and spirituality as two independent constructs, and proposed explanations that included the notion that being religious or having a religious practice was not necessary for a person to be spiritual (Champagne, 2001; Elkins, 1998; Fowler, 1981; Hart, 2003; Kubler-Ross, 1999; Mata, 2015; Miller, 2000; Newberg et al., 2001; Noddings, 2005), I found myself immersed in what is understood as secular spirituality.

Secular spirituality is the adherence to a spiritual philosophy, made evident through spiritual practices, without adherence to a religion. Sheldrake (2013) explains secular spirituality "refers to the varied ways in which the concept of spirituality is increasingly used outside religious contexts" (p. 210). It emphasizes the personal growth and inner peace of the individual, rather than a relationship with the divine. Secular spirituality is comprised of the search for meaning outside of a religious institution; it considers one's relationship with the self, others, nature, and whatever else one considers to be the ultimate (Elkins et al., 1988). Often, the goal of secular spirituality is living happily and/or helping others (Wilkinson, 2007). It emphasizes humanistic qualities such as love, compassion, patience, forgiveness, responsibility, harmony, and concern for others since it is very relational (Lama, 1999). van der Veer (2009) argues aspects of life and human experience which go beyond a purely materialistic view of the world are spiritual; spirituality does not require belief in a supernatural reality or divine being.

In searching for secular definitions of spirituality, I found that spirituality and children's spirituality as it relates to education were defined in four distinct ways. Scholars define spirituality as:

1. **human nature and personal connections and beliefs** (Coles, 1990; Elkins, 1998; Ferguson et al., 2022; Hart, 2003; Haugen, 2018; Hay, 1987; Kessler, 1998/99; Lipton, 2015; McCreery, 1994; Miller, 2021; Newberg et al., 2001; Palmer, 1998/99; Phillips, 2003; Rosenblum & Kuttner, 2011; Scott, 2001, 2003; Tan, 2009);

Defining Spirituality and Differentiating It From Religion

2. **otherness, or unifying and connecting with something other beyond human nature** (Bosacki, 2001; Fowler, 1981; Hart, 2003; Myers & Myers, 1999; Palmer, 2003), **for some including or highlighting the connection to nature or natural source** (Adams & Beauchamp, 2019; Bone, 2007; Harris, 2007);
3. **a combination of the internal aspect (human nature) and the external component (coming from or connecting to something or someone beyond the human being) as being spiritual** (Bellous, 2019; Benson et al., 2003; Berrymann, 1990; Champagne, 2001; de Souza, 2016; Hay & Nye, 2006; Hyde, 2020; Mata, 2015; Parks, 2000; Robinson, 2019; Schein, 2012; Stutts & Schloemann, 2002; Trousdale, 2005a); or as
4. **an essence, a consciousness, and/or a direct sensory awareness, akin to a particular state of mind that allows for being spiritual** (Faver, 2004; Hart, 2003; Hay & Nye, 1998; Johnson, 2006; Lahood, 2010; McCreery, 1994; Miller, 2000; Reimer & Furrow, 2001; Tomlinson et al., 2016). Hay and Nye (2006) call this understanding of spirituality, relational consciousness, and speak of three major categories of spiritual sensitivity through which this relational consciousness manifests: awareness-sensing, mystery-sensing, and value-sensing.

Figure 1.2 offers a summary of the categorization of different authors' definitions of spirituality in these four ways of understanding and defining it. This figure first appeared in my book on spiritual experiences in early childhood education (2015) and has been updated to reflect up-to-date literature in the field.

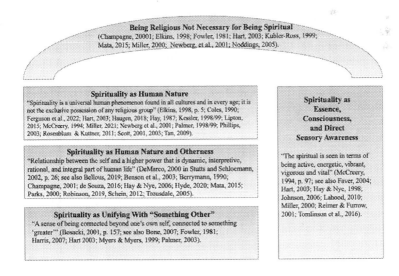

FIGURE 1.2 Definition of spirituality by categories

Source: Jennifer Mata-McMahon

16 What Is Children's Spirituality?

Spirituality as a Holistic View of Development

From a developmental perspective, it seems quite straightforward to include spirituality as another area of development that needs to be addressed when studying or supporting children's developmental progress. When we study child development, typically four main areas are considered: (1) physical and motor, (2) cognitive, (3) language and literacy, and (4) socio-emotional development (Copple & Bredekamp, 2009). Countries that have included spirituality as a required area to be addressed in compulsory educational settings (e.g., Australia, Canada, and the United Kingdom) seem to have tagged along spiritual development to the list of developmental areas needed to be included in curricula and pedagogical strategies implemented to promote learning in schools, leaving teachers the task to determine how to do this in a substantial way that meets the legislative requirements (Bone & Fenton, 2015).

My view of spirituality does not stem from a developmental framework. I view spirituality from a holistic perspective, meaning I understand it to be overarching to all we are as human beings, a result of the interaction of the body, the mind, and the soul. I would agree we can grow and develop the ways in which we express, experience, and connect to the spiritual realm, yet I do not see that progress as determined by stages or occurring in a linear progression, similar to that of the commonly known areas of development. Harald Walach (2017), a medical doctor, scientist, and researcher, supports this notion and explains spirituality can be better understood through the notion of experiences and not stages. For Walach spirituality is composed of spiritual experiences that "are experiences of a reality that is experienced to be beyond the ego and its immediate needs" (p. 7). Through spiritual experiences the human consciousness seems to have direct access to the structure of reality as such, which reflects a similarity to how scientific processes take place: from a deep, often creative insight into the structure behind data to create a theory.

When making the case for spirituality, as spiritual development, to be included in a holistic view of human development, Love and Talbot (1999) describe five propositions that acknowledge a wide range of belief systems that may or may not incorporate organized religion. They further explain some of the propositions, such as "spiritual development's focus on connectedness to self and others, transcending locus of centricity, and deriving meaning, are aspects of traditional psychosocial and cognitive development theory" (p. 617). Yet, they make clear these five propositions are not stages, nor do they present them in a linear or chronological order, further describing these propositions as interrelated and often being evidenced concurrently. The five propositions for spiritual development, according to Love and Talbot (1999), are:

1. an internal process of seeking personal authenticity, genuineness, and wholeness as an aspect of identity development;

Defining Spirituality and Differentiating It From Religion   **17**

2. a process of continually transcending one's current locus of centricity;
3. a greater connectedness to self and others through relationships and union with community;
4. deriving meaning, purpose, and direction in one's life; and
5. an increasing openness to exploring a relationship with an intangible and pervasive power or essence that exists beyond human existence and rational human knowing.

Similarly, when studying spiritual development as it might be nurtured in schools, David Kibble (1996) proposes understanding spiritual development as "a lifelong process of encountering, reflecting on, responding to and developing insight from what, through experience, one perceives to be the trans-personal, transcendent, mystical or numinous. It does not necessarily involve the concept of God" (p. 71).

While the Search Institute (Institute-Search, 2022)[1] defines spiritual development as a constant, ongoing, and dynamic interplay between one's inward journey and one's outward journey, and involving three core developmental processes: (1) awareness and awakening in order to cultivate identity, meaning, and purpose; (2) interconnecting and belonging by seeking and accepting relationships to and interdependence with others; and (3) living an integrated life by authentically expressing one's identity through relationships, activities, and practices shaping oneself and others.

These propositions for spiritual development are well aligned with my understanding of spirituality and bear great resemblance to the definition I propose. From the analysis of the definition of spirituality found in the literature I shared earlier, I define **spirituality as an innate human potential or ability to be fully present in order to connect with ourselves, with others, and with the greater *Other* intangible beyond us, which some call the transcendent or the divine, and others refer to as energy or Spirit.** This connection **affords us the possibility to relate or be in relation with the spiritual realm, and move toward finding meaning and direction in life, rediscovering our purpose as human beings** (Mata, 2015). For me, spirituality has to do with knowing thyself and understanding the reason for living life, as well as with connecting and relating to everything around us (material and spiritual) in a profound and meaningful way.

In the following sections, I explain in more detail what is meant in the literature by each of the components I include in my definition of spirituality: an innate human potential, that allows us to connect and relate to others, in the search for purpose and meaning in life.

Spirituality as an Innate Human Potential or Ability to Be Present

I view spirituality as an innate human ability to be present in order to connect and relate to everything around us. This ability is in the form of a potential we

18 What Is Children's Spirituality?

human beings have that affords us the possibility to connect and to be in relation with spirit and the spiritual realm. We can choose to develop and strengthen this potential, or we can decide to ignore it. It also can be a case of external nourishment that affords us the agency to move toward developing it, or we might be immersed in an environment that hinders and slows down, to the point of non-engagement, our desire and urge to further develop this ability, and in doing so isolates us from the spiritual realm. In my view, we decide whether to engage in spiritual growth or not, it is a choice every one of us can make. The way in which we decide to express our spirituality and live and develop spirituality is also a choice we can make. Haugen (2018) explains this as "spirituality is a fundamental human dimension that exists in modern human beings and has been expressed in different forms in different times, and religion is one form of responding to the need humans have to express their spiritual dimensions" (p. 307). Bellous (2019) agrees,

> I define human spirituality as a sense of felt connection, which is central to a human capacity to survive and thrive . . . the spiritual lies at the foundation of human experience, so that everyone is spiritual, and typically, people use religious language to express spiritual concerns.
>
> *(p. 389)*

Research from the turn of the twenty-first century proposed that humans seem to be 'wired' for spirituality. Newberg et al. (2001) studied the relationship between religious experience and brain function by taking images of the brain, through a SPECT (single-photon emission computed tomography) camera, of eight Tibetan meditators during meditation, and later of several Franciscan nuns at prayer. The scans showed unusual activity in the rear section of the brain, the posterior superior parietal lobe, or what they dubbed "the orientation association area, or OAA" (p. 4). The primary function of the OAA is to orient the individual in physical space, keeping track of angles and distance allowing us to safely negotiate the dangerous physical landscape around us. Put simply, it draws a distinction between the individual and everything else. When the OAA is active, the brain activity appears on the scans as bright reds and yellows. The scans of brains taken at peak meditative states showed the OAA to be bathed in dark blotches of cool greens and blues, indicating a sharp reduction in activity levels.

As their study progressed, the data continued to uncover evidence that the mystical experiences of their "subjects – the altered states of mind they described as the absorption of the self into something larger – were not the result of emotional mistakes or simple wishful thinking" (Newberg et al., 2001), but instead were associated with a series of observable neurological events. These scientists found mystical experiences to be biological, observable, and scientifically real, as they manifested in the human brain. They found evidence of humans having the

Defining Spirituality and Differentiating It From Religion   **19**

ability to connect to the spiritual realm through inherited biological capabilities of their brain; in other words, humans have the innate ability to be spiritual.

Through similar lines of study, Lisa Miller (2021), in her most recent book *The Awakened Brain*, shares findings from her team's neuroscience research searching for the role of spirituality in preventing or protecting against depression. This research showed that using neuroimaging techniques to compare the MRIs (magnetic resonance imaging) of 131 subjects ranging in age from six to 54, with high and low genetic risk for depression, and varying degrees of personal spirituality, a significant difference was detected, indicating that spirituality appears to protect against mental suffering. The findings were astonishing; "the subjects for whom spirituality and religion were highly important had a healthier neural structure than did those for whom spirituality and religion held medium, low, or no importance" (p. 150). Because this study was based on longitudinal data that cut across several generations of subjects, it was able to show how spirituality seems to have a 'buffering effect' against depression when going through developmental windows of risk. "For spiritually aware people across faith traditions – and including those without tradition – the brain appeared able to protect itself from the long-standing neurological structures of depression" (p. 151).

From these findings, Miller (2021) proposes that the awakened brain, as "both inherent to our physiology and invaluable to our health and functioning" (p. 9), includes innate perceptual capacities through which people "experience love and connection, unity, and a sense of guidance from and dialogue with life" (p. 9). This ability each one of us has "to fully develop our innate capacity to live through an awareness of love, interconnection and appreciation of life's unfolding" (p. 10) is what she understands as spirituality.

Other innovative research related to the innateness of spirituality has also been conducted in the fields of biology (Lipton, 2015) and quantum physics (Rosenblum & Kuttner, 2011), showing how spirituality, through quantum energy, manifests itself in the body and in how we understand the physical world around us. In looking to identify neural substrates of spirituality and religiosity, Ferguson et al. (2022) applied lesion network mapping to two independent brain lesion datasets (N_1 = 88; N_2 = 105) to test whether lesion locations were associated with spiritual and religious belief maps. They found that brain lesions associated with self-reported spirituality map onto a brain circuit centered on the periaqueductal grey, a brainstem region previously implicated in fear conditioning, pain modulation, and altruistic behavior. Even with the acknowledged limitations regarding the study participants' religious background (mainly Christian), race and gender (predominantly older white males), and limited definitions of spirituality and religiosity as single behaviors, research studies like these point to the innate quality that spirituality has for human beings, as evidence of it is found in human brains. This innate ability, if chosen to be developed, is what allows humans to connect to self, to others, and to the Other (transcendent or divine) in the spiritual realm.

20 What Is Children's Spirituality?

Spirituality as the Ability to Connect and Relate (to Self, Others, and Other)

When speaking of the spirituality of young children, Kathleen Harris (2007) explains it "involves actively living by being connected to a natural source within the moral universe and affectively belonging with relationships that are interconnected within a child's culture and community" (p. 264). This aspect of connection is commonly found in definitions of spirituality that focus on the person, beyond specifically defining spirituality from a child's perspective. As such, spirituality involves being self-connected and connected to the Other, the source in the spiritual realm, to be able to connect and relate to other beings. Brendan Hyde (2020) agrees with Harris; when defining spirituality, he explains it as "an individual's sense of connectedness and relationship with Self and with everything that is other than Self" (p. 198). While Jane Bone (2007) explains that spirituality connects people to each other, to all living things, to nature, and to the universe, it is a way of appreciating the wonder and mystery of everyday life.

Furthermore, Ann Trousdale (2005b) defines spirituality as "the capacity in human beings for wonderment . . . for interest in the nature and origin of things; and for considering how one is related to others, to oneself, and to the world about us" (p. 63). In this capacity, spirituality is so much more than just following a set of codified beliefs, shared by a community of people, as religion can be understood. James Fowler (1981), the author of the seminal piece *The Stages of Faith*, explains that spirituality is rooted in connectedness, relationship, communion, and community with the spirit and the sense of spirit that often exists in true communities, which is central to his theory of faith development. Likewise, Sharon Parks (2000), the author of *Big Questions, Worthy Dreams: Mentoring Young Adults in Their Search for Meaning, Purpose, and Faith*, also speaks of faith development as the central aspect of spiritual development. Parks (2000) views spirituality to be more of a personal rather than a public search for meaning, transcendence, wholeness, purpose, and apprehension of spirit (or Spirit) as the animating essence at the core of life. She describes spirituality as both immanent (within the individual) and transcendent (beyond the individual). In this sense spirituality, in the experience and activity of faith, both lies beyond the range of ordinary perception and experience and is also ultimately unknowable, remaining within the individual and the particulars of their experience.

When reflecting on spirituality in spaces of teacher education, Parker Palmer (2003) explains, "spirituality is the eternal human yearning to be connected with something larger than our own egos" (p. 377). It seems there is a common thread of understanding the importance of connectedness for humans to be spiritual, to express themselves spiritually, or to engage in spiritual experiences. I would further argue that this connection is what affords us the possibility to better relate, to feel compassion and empathy toward others, and the lack of this ability to connect

Defining Spirituality and Differentiating It From Religion **21**

in order to promote spiritual aspects of ourselves is what makes it difficult for us to fully engage with one another, deepen relationships, and ultimately find meaning and purpose in our existence.

Spirituality to Rediscover Life's Meaning and Purpose

The literature on definitions of spirituality also makes evident scholars who understand the broader role of spirituality as a way for humans to rediscover our life's purpose, and in doing so, living a life of purpose in which the search for meaning and understanding of the bigger questions is of great importance. Urbanowski (1997) highlights succinctly this notion of meaning-making, when he states "spirituality is simply the experiences of meaning" (2003).

England's National Curriculum Council (1988–1993, p. 2) defines spirituality along similar veins,

> as something fundamental in the human condition. . . . It has to do with relationships with other people and, for believers, with God. It has to do with the universal search for individual identity – with our responses to challenging experiences, such as death, suffering, beauty, and encounters with good and evil. It is to do with the search for meaning and purpose in life and for values by which to live.
>
> *(Statham & Webster, 2021)*

In this respect, in his chapter on Religious Education, Spirituality and Anti-racism, Stephen Bigger (2000) offers,

> we need to regard spirituality inclusively as a quest for personal meaning at the highest level, which includes intellectual, ethical, social, political, aesthetic, and other such dimensions. It marks a quality of reflection which is holistic in scope, transcends material needs and ambitions, and transforms the personality in positive ways.
>
> *(p. 33)*

Bellous (2019) further expounds on this by explaining,

> Every human being has a spiritual need to celebrate, mark significant moments, bear witness to truths learned about life, play, tell their story, grieve, mourn, lament, connect with the past, make significant journeys, express themselves symbolically, seek purpose and meaning, ask ultimate questions, have a satisfactory way to think and speak about the beginning and end of life, survive, flourish, experience longing and enjoy its satisfaction, relax, cope with life circumstances, be seen, be heard, have a name that is remembered, be part

22 What Is Children's Spirituality?

of a larger community, organize experience meaningfully so as to make sense of it, maintain human dignity and see the future as hopeful.

(Bellous, 2015, p. 19, in Bellous, 2019, p. 391)

With this list of spiritual needs in mind, we might wonder how we go about satisfying these needs in a fulfilling way. Polemikou and Da Silva (2022) in their review of the literature on children's spirituality found definitions of spirituality that address ways in which these needs might be met. Walton (1996, p. 237) defines spiritual relationships "as relationships to self, others, a higher power, or the environment that bring forth a sense of inner strength, peace, harmonious interconnectedness, and meaning to life" (in Polemikou & Da Silva, 2022, p. 336). While Tan (2009, p. 398) defines spiritual development as "a process of self-transcendence where the individual is an active agent in shaping his or her own spiritual growth" (in Polemikou & Da Silva, 2022, p. 338). And Benson et al. (2003, pp. 205–206) describe spirituality as

the process of growing the intrinsic human capacity for self-transcendence, in which the self is embedded in something greater than the self, including the sacred. It is the developmental 'engine' that propels the search for connectedness, meaning, purpose, and contribution. It is shaped both within and outside of religious traditions, beliefs, and practices.

(In Polemikou & Da Silva, 2022, p. 338)

de Souza et al. (2016) further explain,

the spiritual dimension of life helps individuals create frameworks of meaning and provides individuals with a way of being in the world which influences their decisions and actions. It enables them to interpret their life experiences, which can help them to work through difficult and unhappy times, overcome challenges, and find purpose in being. . . . We have reached a stage in the transitional process of this discipline, then, where we can say that no particular form or expression of spirituality is superior to another, or which can be weighted more favourably [*sic*] than another.

(p. 346)

And lastly, Haugen (2018) adds, spiritual development is "essentially about understanding one's purpose in life and one's overall relationships to self, others, nature and the transcendent, captures in the terms meaning-making, enhanced awareness and connectedness" (p. 318).

This review of the literature offers us evidence of the complexity we encounter while trying to define a term as ethereal as spirituality. Nevertheless, it seems clear from recent research findings that spirituality can be understood as an innate

Defining Spirituality and Differentiating It From Religion **23**

human trait, a potential we can choose to develop or ignore. Yet, as it is embraced it allows us to connect to ourselves, to others around us, to nature, and to the Other beyond the material, the physical realm in which we find ourselves. Viewing human development holistically, including this spiritual potential to connect and relate to others in meaningful ways, provides the opportunity for us to further engage with our purpose and thus find meaning in the lives we live.

Chapter 2 will explore how spirituality is presented in the literature and empirical, applied research as it pertains to children and early childhood education in the past 20 to 30 years, providing a framework for understanding how this phenomenon is understood within the educational context.

Note

1. The Search Institute received support from the John Templeton Foundation to examine the place of spiritual development as a critical domain of positive youth development across traditions and culture.

References

Adams, D., & Beauchamp, G. (2019). Spiritual moments making music in nature: A study exploring the experiences of children making music outdoors, surrounded by nature. *International Journal of Children's Spirituality, 24*(3), 260–275. https://doi.org/10.1080/1364436X.2019.1646220

Bellous, J. E. (2015). *Educating faith: An approach to Christian spiritual formation.* Clements.

Bellous, J. E. (2019). An inclusive spiritual education. *International Journal of Children's Spirituality, 24*(4), 389–400. https://doi.org/10.1080/1364436X.2019.1675603

Benson, P. L., Roehlkepartian, E. C., & Rude, S. P. (2003). Spiritual development in childhood and adolescence: Toward a field of inquiry. *Applied Developmental Science, 7,* 205–213.

Berrymann, J. W. (1990). Teaching as presence and the existential curriculum. *Religious Education, 85*(4), 509–534.

Bigger, S. (2000). Religious education, spirituality and anti-racism. In M. Leicester, S. Mogdil, & S. Mogdil (Eds.), *Spiritual and religious education* (pp. 21–35). Routledge.

Bone, J., & Fenton, A. (2015). Spirituality and child protection in early childhood education: A strengths approach. *International Journal of Children's Spirituality, 20*(2), 86–99. https://doi.org/10.1080/1364436X.2015.1030594

Bone, J. E. (2007). *Everyday spirituality: Supporting the spiritual experience of young children in three early childhood educational settings.* Massey University.

Bosacki, S. L. (2001). Theory of mind or theory of the soul? The role of spirituality in children's understanding of mind and emotions. In J. Erricker, C. Ota, & C. Erricker (Eds.), *Spiritual education: Cultural, religious, and social differences: New perspectives for the 21st century.* Sussex Academic Press.

Champagne, E. (2001). Listening to . . . listening for . . . : A theological reflection on spirituality in early childhood. In J. Erricker, C. Ota, & C. Erricker (Eds.), *Spiritual education: Cultural, religious and social differences: New perspectives for the 21st century.* Sussex Academic Press.

24 What Is Children's Spirituality?

Coles, R. (1990). *The spiritual life of children*. Houghton Mifflin Company.

Copple, C., & Bredekamp, S. (Eds.). (2009). *Developmentally appropriate practice in early childhood programs: Serving children from birth to age 8* (3rd ed.). NAEYC.

de Souza, M. (2016). The spiritual dimension of education – addressing issues of identity and belonging. *Discourse and Communication for Sustainable Education*, 7(1), 125–138. https://doi.org/10.1515/dcse-2016-0009

de Souza, M., Bone, J., & Watson, J. (Eds.). (2016). *Spirituality across disciplines: Research and practice*. Springer International Publishing.

Durkheim, E. (1915). *The elementary forms of religious life*. The Free Press; George, Allen & Unwin Ltd.

Elkins, D. N. (1998). *Beyond religion*. Quest Books Theosophical Publishing House.

Elkins, D. N., Hedstrom, L. J., Hughes, L. L., Leaf, J. A., & Saunders, C. (1988). Toward a humanistic-phenomenological spirituality: Definition, description, and measurement. *Journal of Humanistic Psychology*, 28(4), 5–18.

Faver, C. A. (2004). Relational spirituality and social caregiving. *Social Work*, 49(2), 241. https://doi.org/10.1093/sw/49.2.241

Ferguson, M. A., Schaper, F. L., Cohen, A., Siddiqi, S., Merrill, S. M., Nielsen, J. A., Grafman, J., Urgesi, C., Fabbro, F., & Fox, M. D. (2022). A neural circuit for spirituality and religiosity derived from patients with brain lesions. *Biological Psychiatry*, 91(4), 380–388. https://doi.org/10.1016/j.biopsych.2021.06.016

Fowler, J. W. (1981). *Stages of faith: The psychology of human development and the quest for meaning*. Harper Collins.

Garcia-Romeu, A. (2010). Self-transcendence as a measurable transpersonal construct. *The Journal of Transpersonal Psychology*, 42(1), 26–47.

Hackett, C., Stonawski, M., & McClendon, D. (2017). *The changing global religious landscape*. Pew Research Centre.

Harris, K. I. (2007). Re-conceptualizing spirituality in the light of educating young children. *International Journal of Children's Spirituality*, 12(3), 263–275. https://doi.org/10.1080/13644360701714936

Hart, T. (2003). *The secret spiritual world of children*. Inner Ocean Publishing.

Haugen, H. M. (2018). It is time for a general comment on children's spiritual development. *International Journal of Children's Spirituality*, 23(3), 306–322. https://doi.org/10.1080/1364436X.2018.1487833

Hay, D. (1987). *Exploring inner space*. Mowbray.

Hay, D., & Nye, R. (1998). *The spirit of the child*. Fount.

Hay, D., & Nye, R. (2006). *The spirit of the child* (Revised ed.). Jessica Kingsley Publishers.

Hill, P. C., Pargament, K. I., Hood, J. R. W., McCullough, M. E., Swyers, J. P., Larson, D. B., & Zinnbauer, B. J. (2000). Conceptualizing religion and spirituality: Points of commonality, points of departure. *Journal for the Theory of Social Behaviour*, 30, 51–77. https://doi.org/10.1111/1468-5914.00119

Hyde, B. (2020). Evoking the spiritual through phenomenology: Using the written anecdotes of adults to access children's expressions of spirituality. *International Journal of Children's Spirituality*, 25(3–4), 197–211. https://doi.org/10.1080/1364436X.2020.1843006

Institute-Search. (2022). *Spiritual development*. Search Institute. Retrieved July 14, 2022, from www.search-institute.org/our-research/youth-development-research/spiritual-development/

Johnson, H. (2006). Difference, exploration, certainty and terror: A view from a Londoner about the formation of children's spirituality as relational consciousness.

International Journal of Children's Spirituality, 11(1), 57–70. https://doi.org/10.1080/13644360500503324

Kessler, R. (1999). Nourishing students in secular schools. *Educational Leadership, 49,* 49–52. (Original work published 1998)

Kibble, D. G. (1996). Spiritual development, spiritual experience and spiritual education. In R. Best (Ed.), *Education, spirituality and the whole child.* Cassell.

Koenig, H. G. (1997). *Is religion good for your health? The effects of religion on physical and mental health.* Haworth Pastoral Press.

Kubler-Ross, E. (1999). *The tunnel and the light.* Marlowe & Company.

Lahood, G. (2010). Relational spirituality, part 1. Paradise unbound: Cosmis hybridity and spiritual narcissism in the 'one truth' of new age transpersonalism. *International Journal of Transpersonal Studies, 29*(1), 31–57. https://doi.org/10.24972/ijts.2010.29.1.31

Lama, D. (1999). *Ethics for the new millennium.* Riverhead Books.

Lipton, B. H. (2015). *The biology of belief: Unleashing the power of consciousness, matter and miracles-Bruce H Lipton* (2nd ed.). Hay House, Inc.

Love, P. G. (2000). Differentiating spirituality from religion. *FSU| Character Clearinghouse.* Retrieved March 18, 2022, from https://characterclearinghouse.fsu.edu/article/differentiating-spirituality-religion

Love, P. G., & Talbot, D. (1999). Defining spiritual development: A missing consideration for student affairs. *Journal of Student Affairs Research and Practice, 37*(1), 21–35. https://doi.org/10.2202/1949-6605.1097

Marler, P. L., & Hadaway, C. K. (2002). "Being religious" or "being spiritual" in America: A zero-sum proposition? *Journal for the Scientific Study of Religion, 41,* 289–300.

Mata, J. (2015). *Spiritual experiences in early childhood education: Four kindergarteners, one classroom.* Routledge.

McCreery, E. (1994). Towards an understanding of the notion of the spiritual in education. *Early Child Development and Care, 100,* 93–99. https://doi.org/10.1080/0300443941000106

Miller, J. S. (2000). *Direct connection: Transformation of consciousness.* Routledge Books, Inc.

Miller, L. (2021). *The awakened brain: The new science of spirituality and our quest for an inspired life.* Random House.

Myers, B. K., & Myers, M. E. (1999). Engaging children's spirit and spirituality through literature. *Childhood Education, 76*(1), 28–32.

National Curriculum Council. (1988–1993). *Records of the National Curriculum Council.* The National Archives.

Newberg, A., D'Aquili, E., & Rause, V. (2001). *Why God won't go away: Brain science and the biology of belief.* Ballantine Books.

Noddings, N. (2005). *Happiness and education.* Cambridge University Press.

Palmer, P. J. (1998/1999). Evoking the spirit in public education. *Educational Leadership, 6,* 6–12.

Palmer, P. J. (2003). Teaching with heart and soul: Reflections on spirituality in teacher education. *Journal of Teacher Education, 54*(5), 376–385. https://doi.org/10.1177/0022487103257359

Parks, S. D. (2000). *Big questions, worthy dreams: Mentoring young adults in their search for meaning, purpose, and faith.* Jossey-Bass.

Phillips, I. (2003). Infusing spirituality into geriatric health care: Practical applications from the literature. *Topics in Geriatric Rehabilitation, 19*(4), 249–256.

26 What Is Children's Spirituality?

Polemikou, A., & Da Silva, J. P. (2022). Readdressing spiritual growth: What can we learn from childhood education? *Journal of Humanistic Psychology*, *62*(3), 334–351. https://doi.org/10.1177/0022167820938612

Reimer, K., & Furrow, J. (2001). A qualitative exploration of relational consciousness in Christian children. *International Journal of Children's Spirituality*, *6*(1), 7–23. https://doi.org/10.1080/13644360124074

Robinson, C. (2019). Young children's spirituality: A focus on engaging with nature. *Australasian Journal of Early Childhood*, *44*(4), 339–350. https://doi.org/10.1177/1836939119870907

Rosenblum, B., & Kuttner, F. (2011). *Quantum enigma: Physics encounters consciousness.* Oxford University Press.

Sagberg, S. (2006). Teachers' lives as wonder journeys: Ethical reflections on spirituality in education. In K. Tirri (Ed.), *Nordic perspectives on religion, spirituality and identity: Yearbook 2006 of the Department of Practical Theology* (pp. 286–300). University of Helsinki, Department of Practical Theology.

Schein, D. (2012). *Early childhood educators' perceptions of spiritual development in young children: A social constructivist grounded theory study* [Doctoral Dissertation, Walden University].

Schlehofer, M. M., Omoto, A. M., & Adelman, J. R. (2008). How do "religion" and "spirituality" differ? Lay definitions among older adults. *Journal for the Scientific Study of Religion*, *47*(3), 411–425.

Scott, D. (2001). Storytelling, voice and qualitative research: Spirituality as a site of ambiguity and difficulty. In J. Erricker, C. Ota, & C. Erricker (Eds.), *Spiritual education: Cultural, religious, and social differences: New perspectives for the 21st century.* Sussex Academic Press.

Scott, D. G. (2003). Spirituality in child and youth care: Considering spiritual development and "relational consciousness". *Child & Youth*, *32*(2), 117–131. https://doi.org/10.1023/A:1022593103824

Sheldrake, P. (2013). *Spirituality: A brief history* (2nd ed.). Wiley-Blackwell.

Smith, L. S. (2007). *The illustrated timeline of religion: A crash course in words & pictures.* Sterling.

Statham, A., & Webster, R. S. (2021). Engaging with Dewey's valuation in religious education to enhance children's spirituality for democratic life. *Religions*, *12*(8), 629. https://doi.org/10.3390/rel12080629

Stutts, A., & Schloemann, J. (2002). Life-sustaining support: Ethical, cultural and spiritual conflicts Part I: Family support – a neonatal case study. *Neonatal Network*, *21*(3), 23–29. https://doi.org/10.1891/0730-0832.21.4.27

Tan, C. (2009). Reflection for spiritual development in adolescents. In M. D. Souza, L. J. Francis, J. O'Higgins-Norman, & D. Scott (Eds.), *International handbook of education for spirituality, care and wellbeing* (Vol. 3, pp. 397–413). Springer. https://doi.org/10.1007/978-1-4020-9018-9_22

Tomlinson, J., Glenn, E. S., Paine, D. R., & Sandage, S. J. (2016). What is the "relational" in relational spirituality? A review of definitions and research directions. *Journal of Spirituality in Mental Health*, *18*(1), 55–75. https://doi.org/10.1080/19349637.2015.1066736

Trousdale, A. M. (2005a). "And what do children say?" Children's responses to books about spiritual matters. In C. Ota & C. Erricker (Eds.), *Spiritual education: Literary, empirical and pedagogical approaches* (pp. 23–39). Sussex Academic Press.

Trousdale, A. M. (2005b). Intersections of spirituality, religion and gender in children's literature. *International Journal of Children's Spirituality*, *10*(1), 61–79. https://doi.org/10.1080/13644360500039709

Turner, R. P., Lukoff, D., Barnhouse, R. T., & Lu, F. G. (1995). Religious or spiritual problem: A culturally sensitive diagnostic category in the DSM-IV. *Journal of Nervous and Mental Disease, 183*, 435–444.

Urbanowski, R. (1997). *Spirituality in everyday practice: Finds that defining spirituality as "the experience of meaning" allows practitioners and their clients to add an important dimension to the therapeutic process* (Vol. 2, pp. 18–23.). OT Practice.

van der Veer, P. (2009). Spirituality in modern society. *Social Research: An International Quarterly, 76*(4), 1097–1120.

Van Niekerk, B. (2018). Religion and spirituality: What are the fundamental differences? *HTS: Theological Studies, 74*(3), 1–11. https://hdl.handle.net/10520/EJC-ec668076f

Walach, H. (2017). Secular spirituality – what it is. Why we need it. How to proceed. *Journal for the Study of Spirituality, 7*(1), 7–20.

Walton, J. (1996). Spiritual relationships: A concept analysis. *Journal of Holistic Nursing, 14*(3), 237–250. https://doi.org/10.1177/089801019601400306

Wilkinson, T. (2007). *The lost art of being happy: Spirituality for sceptics.* Findhorn Press.

Wunn, I. (2000). Beginning of religion. *Numen, 47*(4), 417–452.

Zinnbauer, B. J., Pargament, K. I., Cole, B., Rye, M. S., Butter, E. M., Belavich, T. G., Hipp, K. M., & Kadar, J. L. (1997). Religion and spirituality: Unfuzzying the fuzzy. *Journal for the Scientific Study of Religion, 36*(4), 549–564.

Zinnbauer, B. J., Pargament, K. I., & Scott, A. B. (1999). The emerging meanings of religiousness and spirituality: Problems and prospects. *Journal of Personality, 67*, 889–919.

2

UNDERSTANDING CHILDREN'S SPIRITUALITY IN THE LITERATURE AND RESEARCH

When I became interested in children's spirituality as a field of inquiry and research in 2005, it was still an underexplored and quite niche area of study. Robert Coles' book *The Spiritual Lives of Children* (1990) and a seminal piece by David Hay and Rebecca Nye published in 1996 as a doctoral dissertation, and then revised and published as a book, *The Spiritual Child* (2006), were the only foundational works researchers had to begin empirical explorations in this topic. In 2016, I published an article on the review of the empirical research on children's spirituality from 2005 to 2015 (Mata-McMahon, 2016), to date one of my most cited publications. For this article, I was able to only find under a dozen empirical studies conducted with children ages zero to eight, of which one of them was the study I conducted with four kindergarteners in 2010; this study is presented in my book, *Spiritual Experiences in Early Childhood Education* (2015).

I began my review of the research on children's spirituality stemming from the work advanced by Ratcliff (2010). In presenting a review of scholarly studies on children's spiritual and religious development, he identified four salient phases for this work. (1) An early holistic period (1892–1930), followed by (2) an era of decreased emphasis upon experiences (1930–1960), continued by (3) three decades of emphasis upon cognitive stages (1960–1990), culminating in (4) a shift of interest toward children's spirituality (1990–2010). Ratcliff's (2008) review highlighted Robinson's (1977) work examining adult retrospective accounts of their religious experiences as children; Coles' (1990) findings from interviewing 500 children between ages eight and 12, using largely a narrative approach to compare accounts of children from different religious backgrounds; and lastly, Hay and Nye's (2006) grounded theory work, interviewing 38 children ages six to 11, looking into defining children's spirituality, arriving at the notion of three types

DOI: 10.4324/9781003081463-4

of spiritual sensitivity (i.e., awareness-sensing, mystery-sensing, and value-sensing) leading into the proposed construct of spirituality as relational consciousness. Ratcliff (2010) highlights these studies as seminal works, representing the thinking of each of the decades in which they were published.

My review in 2016 looked to expand Ratcliff's work by examining the most current empirical research on children's spirituality, specifically focusing on applied studies with children (ages zero to eight) as participants. Not having much luck with the studies being found, I had to extend the age range of the study participants to 12 in order to increase the sample of the works reviewed, and still, I found fewer than 15 studies that I later grouped into three main categories: (1) studies looking into children's spiritual meaning-making and the relationship to or with God (Fisher, 2015; Hay & Nye, 2006; Mitchell et al., 2012; Moore et al., 2011, 2012); (2) studies pertaining to children's spirituality in education and/or educational settings (Bone, 2005; Hyde, 2008; Mata, 2015; Mountain, 2007; Wills, 2011); and (3) studies looking into children's identity formation and the sense of self through engaging with spirituality (Gunnestad & Thwala, 2011; Holder et al., 2010; Moriarty, 2011; Yeung & Chow, 2010).

Expanding on my review from 2016 to include recent empirical research conducted with children and spirituality has shown a steady growth in the body of work, yet made evident this field is still under-researched. I was able to find only ten new studies conducted with children ages zero to eight, and nine more studies that included older children, up to 11, 14, and 18 years of age, adding to the original 15 studies I reviewed in 2016.[1]

Studies on Children's Spiritual Meaning-Making and Relationships (Including to/with God)

In exploring how mother–infant interactions during musical activities for infants in church spaces support spirituality, Kilpeläinen and Ruokonen (2018) conducted a case study of the baby hymn singing (BHS) meetings in the Evangelical Lutheran Church in Denmark. They looked specifically at the seventh session of eight BHS meetings, particularly at the second participating group, constituting seven mothers and their four- to five-month-old infants. Through video recording, observations, and interviews, the researchers found four types of human interaction: mother–infant interaction, interaction between the participants, interaction between the participants and instructors, and ritual interaction. Kilpeläinen and Ruokonen concluded that BHS can be seen as a space for (spi)ritual interaction and, in this context, nurturing spirituality, combined with religious elements.

Furthermore, BHS was found to support infants' spirituality, understood as relational and connectedness, by facilitating not only mother–infant interactions but also nurtured by interactions with other mothers and infants. The ritual interactions offered another layer of spiritual support for infants, as the participants

30 What Is Children's Spirituality?

created a relationship with the BHS environment in which spirituality was nurtured through rituals, hymns, and prayers, and in turn with their cultural heritage, particularly the Danish Christian culture. This type of spiritual support through ritual interactions resulted in what Yust (2003) calls religious enculturation, "the immersion of persons within a ritual community that has a clearly defined narrative tradition and identity, coupled with a set of personal and social ethical norms" (p. 148) and makes evident how intentionally planned activities can support and nurture infants' spiritual development through social interactions.

Another case study conducted in Scandinavia, this time in Norway, also looked at spirituality from a cultural and relational perspective. Steinholt (2007) studied preschool age children (two- to four-year-old) invited to explore a small chapel, a 'sacred space', and participate in a drama and theater performance called 'Speranza's journey', based on a girl searching for her father. From this study, Steinholt (2007) found that (1) even small children are capable of transcending time and space in search for meaning; this was made visible, prompted by the chapel as a space that incited intense sensory experiences, exemplified by a small boy whose parents were going through a marriage separation, and who spontaneously placed his sorrow in the chapel by prostrating himself by the altar, giving himself up to someone stronger, or to mercy. Likewise, findings also pointed to (2) surroundings, in this specific case the chapel, providing an intentional framework for experiences and expressions of the spirit to manifest, highlighting the importance of what surrounds us in delimiting or empowering the ways in which children define themselves. And lastly, (3) the chapel experience illustrated how children felt empowered by symbols of a spiritual world in situations of pain and tension. Sagberg (2008) recognizes these findings as evidence of "how giving children open access to a chapel, to sacred space, is one way of being hospitable to them as spiritual beings" (p. 360), providing them with recognition and respect. This type of experience could be replicable in school settings, provided that schools could be considered places in which children could experience the sacred.

Kathy Frady (2019) conducted a similar study in the U.S., this one with 20 two-year-old children in a setting that offered what she considered necessary for young children to explore their spiritual and theological ideas. Frady proposes a framework, scaffolding, and language as the needed backdrop to children's play interactions in order to capture theological understanding from the child's point of view. Using the program *Godly Play* through a grounded theory approach, allowing for the emergence of the concept of facilitating theology with two-year-old children, which she termed 'rendering theology'. The sub-themes she found for the young children's incipient theology included: eager receptiveness, pretending to read the Bible play, and Jesus play, consisting of reenacting an adaptation of the story of Jesus and the children, from Mark 10:13–16, using wooden figures and props. This study

Understanding Children's Spirituality in the Literature and Research **31**

gives light on not only a theory regarding very young children's theological ideas but also a spiritual qualitative methodology that may be used for future research with two-year-old children, particularly for studies focused on Christian theological understandings of spirituality.

Another study with children ages between three and five in the West Coast of Canada, looking into post-structural interpretations and a hermeneutical phenomenological recounting of an experience of inquiring about angels with young children, collected through observations and focus group discussions, revealed the area of invisible mystery to be more delicate to negotiate than the world of physical embodiments and the world of complete fantasy of the mind. The area of the spiritual represented the meeting of body and mind with a third and overlapping space, the spiritual space, which remained indefinable and intangible. During this study, Pettersen (2015) found that meaning did come through the inquiring and also through the themes that emerged of 'who we are' in relation to angels, race, gender, and the role of the nurturer, as well as through familial angel ownership, such as angels perceived as deceased grandparents and parents. She observed that children yearned for allowing spaces to safely express their ideas about, and experiences with, mystery and spiritual worlds. Pettersen explains that it is this connection with the inner life through small moments and engagements with the big life questions where the entangling of the physical, the mental, and the spiritual creates the intuitive, integrated heart space holistic pedagogy, that will support children's spiritual development. Teachers could provide opportunities for these pondering of big ideas and questions to nurture their students' spirit.

Lastly, a qualitative study involving text reading and movie viewing, conducted in Sweden with 40 six- to nine-year-old children in two different elementary schools, looked to identify children's values and how these values inform their life goals, which the authors comprehend as a reflection of children's understanding of purpose and meaning in life (Ristiniemi & Ahmadi, 2021). The findings showed that these children perceive togetherness, kindness, fairness, and freedom as child-specific values, and wealth and family to be societal-specific values. The researchers noticed that there seemed to be a value differentiation in children's thinking. They explained, "these child-specific values seem to go with meaning in life or that which makes life worth living. It is not money that makes life worth living, but relational values (values in relationships)" (p. 59) which are of importance to these children. These findings seem to reflect time- and society-specific ideas, widely spread in Sweden, in which material values toward money result in greed, injustice, and selfishness. The children also noted that they found more injustice and poverty abroad and society needed to "work to help those countries . . . to create a more just world" (p. 59). Regarding goals in life, children spoke of heaven and hell, believing good people go to heaven and bad people go to hell. Their

32 What Is Children's Spirituality?

goals in life seemed to be better aligned with the child-centered values, of "living together and taking care of each other" (p. 64). Justice and fairness also seemed to be at the center of children's values; they shared

> things such as: all people are equal, people should be together, no one is to be left alone, the needs and integrity of the person are to be respected (if s/he does not want to speak with the teacher, the choice is his or hers), no one should have an excess of money, even a criminal deserves empathy (we could shoot him in the leg instead of pronouncing the death penalty).
>
> *(p. 64)*

This study is a good example of how the social environment in which children find themselves can determine the values they hold, and in turn how they behave and relate to others around them. As we think of children holistically, including moments of reflection on how we relate and treat others could help children inform their purpose in life and support their spiritual development.

Other studies focusing on children as research subjects or participants centered on older children, from eight or nine to 11 years of age. A qualitative study conducted in the East of England with 44 children ages eight to 11 interviewed at school found that children reported experiencing both positive and dark spiritual experiences after visiting a sacred space. Pauline Lovelock and Kate Adams (2017) found three key themes arising from their conversations with the children: (1) divine encounter (e.g., direct communication with God or angels, divine presence through Jesus, angels, or deceased relatives), (2) physical feelings (e.g., rise in temperature, tingling sensation, butterflies in their stomach, glazed eyes, feeling 'beyond time'), and (3) fear (e.g., fear of encountering the devil, having God speak to them, seeing ghosts or dead people). From the children's reports, they concluded that in supporting children's spirituality, it is important to recognize both the light and dark and the blurred boundaries between them, in addition to different ways of perceiving them, to understand the whole child. These findings are important since they move from the tendency to understand spirituality as only love and light and call attention to the dark or fearful side of spirituality providing insights into how children navigate these aspects for adults who seek to support them.

Another study conducted with eight- to 11-year-olds, in KwaZulu, South Africa, examined children's conceptions of spirituality through drawings, writing letters to God, and answering questions on vignettes and scenarios containing moral dilemmas (Hlatshwayo et al., 2018). The study found three salient themes from their emerging conceptions of spirituality: (1) conceptions of a transcendental being; (2) spirituality as a search for personal meanings; and (3) influences on emerging conceptions of spirituality. For these children, being spiritual was about connecting with a transcendental being and with significant others in their lives through expressions of love, respect, hope, faith, compassion, closeness, fairness, and empathy. Children appeared to acquire a sense of spirituality mainly by internalizing experiential

Understanding Children's Spirituality in the Literature and Research **33**

interactions within their social and material environment. Studies like this should be further explored with younger children to offer insight to parents and teachers as to how to best support children's conceptualization of spirituality through providing nurturing experiences and a spiritually encouraging environment.

Lastly, a large study conducted with a sample of 1,328 students ages eight to 11, from Wales, used a modified version of the Fisher 16-item Feeling Good, Living Life measure of spiritual well-being (assessing quality of relationships across four domains: self, family, nature, and God), alongside measures of frequency of worship attendance and frequency of personal prayer, to explore the relationship between prayer, worship, and spiritual well-being for children (Francis et al., 2018). Findings demonstrated frequency of personal prayer was a much stronger predictor than frequency of worship attendance in respect to spiritual well-being. This finding is consistent with the view that personal prayer is a key factor in the formation of individual spirituality and supports spiritual practices, which could be encouraged in secular settings, as ways to nurture spiritual well-being beyond traditional religious ones.

Studies on Children's Spirituality in Education/ Educational Settings

In searching for studies conducted with children in educational settings to investigate aspects of their spirituality, I was able to find only a few. One was a recent hermeneutic phenomenological study conducted with 15 four- to five-year-old children at a nursery school in Potchefstroom, South Africa (Nortjé & Van der Merwe, 2016). This study looked to reveal the meanings children ascribe to their experiences of connectedness in a group music class. Data were collected by means of interviews, close observations, diaries, and drawings. Findings showed emerging themes regarding children's experiences in music class pertaining to children's love of music, the effects music had in their minds, bodies, and emotions, and sharing the musical experience with others in the group. This study demonstrated how music group classes in early childhood education could be useful in creating opportunities for spiritual experiences, promoting connectedness, and consequently fostering children's spiritual well-being.

Another qualitative ethnographic study conducted with four- to five-year-olds from two kindergartens (one Catholic and one Islamic) in Vienna, Austria (Stockinger, 2019), found that depending on their religious background, children have different opportunities to develop their spiritual communication and spirituality based on their specific religious traditions and rituals. Developing kindergarten classrooms in line with the metaphor of safe spaces where diversity is recognized and discussed can contribute to the creation of equal opportunities for children's spiritual development.

Safe spaces can stand metaphorically for spaces of learning, belonging, and recognition of difference. In safe spaces, children feel that their differences are

34 What Is Children's Spirituality?

listened to and acknowledged, they are encouraged to address issues that concern them and there is a sensitive confrontation with differences. In this way, children find a space in which they can develop their spirituality because they know that they can learn with and from each other, and that they belong and are recognized.

(Stockinger, 2019, p. 314)

This study found that although kindergarten directors talk about inclusivity and religious plurality, they teach one religion in their respective schools based on their faith. The observations, interviews, and group discussions combined showed that the way religion is addressed and how religious differences are dealt with aligns with the major dominating religion, while the recognition of minor religions and beliefs is limited. The major religion shapes everyday life, and the recognizability of religious differences is mainly avoided. The children of the minor religions and beliefs tend to be unable to experience their own religion as an enrichment but exclusively as a deficit. Nevertheless, children have the desire to belong to the kindergarten class in which the major religion dominates; children of the minor religions and beliefs express this by not addressing their own religious or spiritual feelings and adapting their behavior to that of children of the major religion. From studies like this, it becomes evident that the development of children's spirituality must not be viewed in isolation, and in fact, the development of spirituality can be influenced by the context. Even though spirituality develops individually, it is important to consider the conditions that facilitate or complicate such development and be aware of how we can not only celebrate, and accept, but also include differences in spiritual beliefs and practices in the classroom.

Other studies with older children, focused on how 70 seven- to 11-year-old children from Irish primary schools, describe the deep fruits of meditation in their lives after practicing it at school for over two years (Keating, 2017b). Findings showed that children can and do enjoy deep states of consciousness and that meditation has the capacity to nourish the innate spirituality of the child.

The subtle language of the children reveals how meditation seems to lead the children to a kind of insightful knowledge, which inspires them to respond rather than react to situations they encounter; as if somehow, deep within the psyche, they have come to understand what response the particular situation calls for and they act on that wisdom rather than react based on their own egoic concerns. Although it may seem paradoxical, it seems that the practice of self-forgetfulness leads to a growing sense of self-responsibility and the capacity to act on it.

(Keating, 2017b, p. 9)

Understanding Children's Spirituality in the Literature and Research **35**

Meditation was found to help children be kinder to others, brought them closer to God, helped them feel the goodness inside, and ultimately helped them be more self-aware, accept themselves for who they really are, as well as others (Keating, 2017a). Studies like this highlight the importance of personal spiritual experience for children and support the introduction of meditation in primary schools to support children's spiritual development.

An interesting study for its rarity was a two-year experimental study with 3,278 children ages 10–14, from schools in 15 countries, who underwent a spiritual education program (SEP) aimed at enhancing altruism and prosocial behavior (Pandya, 2017). To design the SEP, four experts from four faith-based international organizations came together to develop the objectives for the program, select themes that adequately incorporated diversity, prepare a set of activities and experiential exercises, and prepare a general modus operandi to operationalize the program through the help of spiritual trainers associated with their spiritual organizations based in different countries. The SEP comprised two-hour sessions for three days, repeated once every quarter, for a total of eight times in the span of two years. One round comprised the three two-hour lessons conducted over a period of three days; a minimum of five rounds were required to gain participant status in the study. Rounds six through eight were optional.

The three-day two-hour per day lessons included the themes of (1) relational consciousness (respecting the I and the other); (2) dispositional and situational empathy; and (3) unconditional love and forgiveness. These themes were facilitated through a combination of lectures, multi-media content, and experiential or do-it-yourself practical exercises. At the end of each lesson participants were given take-home exercises and points to ponder related to the exercises completed during the lessons. The 180 trainers were selected from the participating faith-based organizations, based on their experience conducting programs for children, and were trained by the experts. Most trainers were women (79%), all had university degrees, and 10 or more years as trainers for the spiritual organization with which they were affiliated (Christian, Hindu-inspired, or Buddhist).

Results showed that post-test scores of the participant children on the self-report altruism scale and prosocial personality battery were higher than the comparison group, and their own pre-test scores. Participant children from affluent countries, high scorers on self-reported religiosity and spirituality, and those who attended six-eight rounds of the SEP and regularly self-practiced had higher post-treatment scores. Hierarchical regression models showed that self-practice was the most important post-test predictor of altruism and prosocial behavior. This study is interesting as it reflects how spirituality can be intentionally supported, through carefully designed educational programs with curricula focused on altruistic and prosocial behaviors, which in turn reinforce their connections to and relationships with self and others.[2]

36 What Is Children's Spirituality?

Studies on Children's Identity Formation and Sense of Self Through Spirituality

Studies exploring children's identity formation and looking into their sense of self through spiritual experiences or expressions, focusing directly on children as study participants, seem to be found in more abundance. Recently published, *The Bloomsbury Handbook of Culture and Identity from Early Childhood to Early Adulthood* (2021), presents a series of studies conducted across the world that look into children and youth's sense of identity from a cultural (Eaude, 2019, 2021; Farrugia, 2021; Ilisko, 2021; Rawi & Letchamanan, 2021), religious (Buchanan, 2021; Davids, 2021; Gulamhusein, 2021; Katz, 2021; Roux & Becker, 2021), and spiritual (Gross, 2021; Hart, 2021; London, 2021) perspective.

Earlier works, like Gill Goodliff's (2013) ethnographic study with 20 children ages between two and four in a secular setting in an urban community in the midlands area of England, also look into how children's identity is expressed through spiritual expressions. Data recorded through field notes, observations, audio recordings of children's conversations and spontaneous expressions, digital photographs, and digital filming were analyzed through a framework based on the literature, including four interrelating dimensions:

1. relational (connectedness to others);
2. reflective (meaning making of individual experience)
3. creative (imaginative play, questioning, expressive arts); and
4. transcendent (awe and wonder, mystery).

In the article reviewed, particularly focusing on three of the children studied, findings showed these children expressed their spirituality primarily through the dimension Creative, specifically through imaginative play, including child-initiated role-play and collaborative play. These findings highlight the importance of fostering creativity through free, imaginative, pretend play for younger children, particularly because creating and imagining are central for children to express their thinking, make meaning of the world around them, and negotiate their identities. Studies like this advocate for the importance to keep early childhood curricula child-centered and open-ended, allowing for creativity to develop as it supports the whole child, and fosters children's spiritual development.

Another study focused on identity and the sense of self was conducted by Kathleen Harris (2018), who explored several personae the spiritual child typically assumes, prompted by learning using technology, specifically tablets, as a component for understanding children's spirituality. This exploratory study summarizes 20 children's (aged 3–5) perceptions and 14 early childhood student educators' reflections of photos taken by young children using tablets while exploring nature and the outdoors at a child development lab school in the U.S. Midwest.

Digital photos using tablets and taken by young children encouraged connections and descriptive conversations about their world and provided a framework for future early childhood educators to consider while regarding the spiritual domain through children's eyes. Findings showed the children expressing their spiritual essence through personae related to: (1) the dramatist filled with wonder, (2) the naturalist and visionary seeing beauty in life, (3) the creative artist, and (4) the awakener of transformative learning, making evident that the child's soul can be nurtured through cooperative learning, creative thinking, and personal reflection (Hart, 2011).

A non-experimental study conducted in Indonesia with 106 elementary school–aged children (ages 9–12) looking into a correlation between spirituality and resilience is another example of research exploring children's sense of self in the world through spirituality. Nauli and Mulyono (2019) adapted the Multidimensional Measure of Religiousness/Spirituality (MRS) containing 12 questions from 11 domains measuring religious/spiritual value. To measure emotional resilience, the researchers adapted a measure used with humanities faculty and students and developed a questionnaire with 14 age-appropriate questions. Findings showed 60% of the children had high spirituality levels, and 56% had positive emotional resilience; when the two variables were correlated, it was found that 39% of children had both high levels of spirituality and positive emotional resilience. Though further research needs to be completed and instruments developed to specifically measure this age group's spirituality, the researchers concluded that "there is a significant relationship between spirituality and emotional endurance in children, which means that spirituality influences the formation of children's emotional resilience" (p. 144), and thus "spirituality cannot be separated from one's life . . . [it] is a child's basic need that must be met for the formation of emotional resilience, and is used as a tool to improve children's mental health" (p. 144).

Another study with somewhat older children (ages 10–18) in Australia explored the ethnic identity formation of Coptic students enrolled in faith-based schools managing their student's well-being through pastoral care. Mansour and Moloney (2020) surveyed 326 students using scales widely employed in older ethnicity studies and selected items related to student's attitude to identity, acculturation, and religiosity, including six items from the Multigroup Ethnic Identity Measure (MEIM). They also conducted focus groups with 41 students, exploring perceptions of Coptic heritage, the school, and their own negotiations of identity. Findings showed, "students negotiated many complexities within two different forces: a sense of heritage and sense of belonging also in the broader community in Australia" (p. 57). "Students' sense of belonging to both the wider community, and the smaller school, church, and diaspora communities, allows them diverse opportunities to develop in multiple identity formation" (p. 61). These students seemed to be navigating many identities as young Australians. The findings highlighted

38 What Is Children's Spirituality?

the importance of culture, language, religion, and overall spirituality in identity formation, and alerting both school and community to the developmental benefits, particularly to self-confidence and self-esteem, afforded by understanding the tension between maintaining cultures of ethnic origin and new, normalized fluid processes of identity experience. School curriculum and welfare policies need to meet the challenge of positively supporting children and youth in balancing intersecting identities. These findings can certainly be extrapolated to other countries with similarly diverse student populations.

When looking to understand children's spirituality, Brendan Hyde (2018) conducted a phenomenological study focusing on pathic knowing, a form of non-cognitive knowledge emanating from the body, through four modalities – actional knowing, situational knowing, relational knowing, and corporeal knowing. Hyde explains that "the pathically tuned body is able to recognize itself in its responsiveness to the things of the lifeworld and to others who share that world" (p. 348). The pathic sense perceives the world in feeling and is what Heidegger (1962) explained as a felt understanding people have of themselves in situations. Others have termed this type of knowing as the subject of the body (Merleau-Ponty, 1962) or as body knowing (Berryman, 2013).

Hyde (2018) used this lens, focused on pathic knowing, for the analysis of the data on a 10-year-old girl from a rural part of Australia, who was a participant in his larger study looking to determine characteristics of children's spirituality. The pathic knowing analysis was conducted on a story the girl shared with her peers and the researcher during a focus group activity. In her narrative, the girl shared she had experienced her deceased sister both in dreams and during a visit to a location frequented by the family when the sister was in life. From the phenomenological analysis of the story shared by the girl, Hyde determined that the girl was able to use her actional, bodily knowledge to assist her in addressing issues of meaning and value and to cope with the loss of her sister. She was able to use the death of her sister[3] and her experiences of her sister after death, to cope with and to address issues of meaning and value in her life, as the experiences resulted in absolute certainty for her, becoming a part of her being (Priestley, 2001). The girl had embodied the experience and it now resided in her actions and her body. Moving forward, this experience would inform her understanding of her relationship with others as well as her understanding of the relationship between the living and the dead.

Hyde's study is particularly interesting because it highlights the importance of spiritual experiences as they inform children's identity, particularly when these experiences are shared and understood beyond a materialist paradigm,[4] and the framework used to comprehend them is expanded to include other ways of knowing such as a pathic knowing worldview.

Lastly, a larger study looking to identify the social-psychological conditions for the formation of ideas about the spiritual ideal for primary school-aged children

(Pomytkina et al., 2019) convened 180 students (108 girls and 72 boys) aged 7–8 (52), 9 (66), and 10–11 years old (62), 80 parents, and 20 teachers. The data were collected through observation sessions (720), responses received with the projective method 'Fairy World' implemented in conversations (1080), children's drawings analyzed by the projective method 'Study of the characteristics of the child identification' (80), and parents (880) and teachers (220) responses. The data were analyzed searching for value-positive attitude to the ideals of beauty and good, and to identify the bearers of these ideals. Pomytkina et al. (2019) found that younger children were more interested in the activities of other children and eager to take part in them during both lessons and their free time, than older participating students. Also, the number of boys who wanted to work with class-mates in their free time was found higher than that of girls. Boys were found to be more likely to become acquainted with each other, find common interests, and play group sports with peers from other grades, than girls, who tended to com-municate in dyads or triads with close friends. Regarding beauty and goodness, they found that "children named it beautiful when something delighted them, made them anxious, joyful, enthusiastic and interested, when it delivered aesthetic pleasure" (p. 378), and consequently, they called it ugly when something caused a negative perception. Overall findings identified the factors influencing the for-mation of the spiritual ideal and socio-psychological conditions of its formation as the peculiarities of relationships with others (parents, teachers, friends, peers, acquaintances, and strangers); influence of mass media (TV products, computer network, radio information, books, literary works, magazines, newspapers); and artistic aesthetic influence (works of art and theatre, communication with nature, aesthetic priorities and preferences, artistic amateur activities). These findings point to the importance of providing children with nurturing and supportive relationships, having parents carefully monitor the quality of children's screen and media consumption, as well as their engagement and participation in artistic experiences.

The review of this empirical research focusing on children as participants has furthered the field of children's spirituality in promoting the understanding of how children make meaning and relate to others spiritually, how children's spirituality is being supported in educational settings, and how children's iden-tity formation and sense of self can be comprehended through the lens of spir-ituality. However, the small number of studies available also shows how much more research is still needed to better gauge how young children experience and express themselves spiritually (Mata, 2015). A more comprehensive and pluralis-tic approach to this research is needed, including children from all corners of the world, representing all faiths and belief systems, races, ethnicities, and languages, to better inform parents, caregivers, teachers, educators, and adults in general how to best support and nurture children holistically, as they continue to develop spiritually.

40 What Is Children's Spirituality?

Notes

1. These studies' foci could be grouped in the same categories established before and will be explained subsequently.
2. Other studies found under this category of looking at spirituality in education or educational settings focused on teachers and center directors who work directly with young children, yet did not have children as the study participants. Some of these studies will be shared in Chapter 6 when speaking to how spirituality can be supported in the early childhood classroom, specifically in secular settings.
3. This is an example of what Maslow, A. (1970), *Religions, Values and Peak-Experiences*. Viking Press, named 'peak experience'; Robinson, E. (1977), *The Original Vision: A Study of the Religious Experience of Childhood*, Religious Experience Research Unit, termed 'original experience'; and James, J. (1997), The talented tenth recalled, in J. James (Ed.), *Transcending the Talented Tenth* (pp. 15–34), Routledge, first proposed as 'religious experience', now more commonly understood as spiritual experience.
4. Materialism, also called physicalism, in philosophy, consists of the view that all facts (including facts about the human mind and will and the course of human history) are causally dependent upon physical processes, or even reducible to them (Smart, 2022). Smart, J. J. C. (July 25, 2022). Materialism. *Encyclopedia Britannica*. https://www.britannica.com/topic/materialism-philosophy

References

Berryman, J. W. (2013). Spirituality, religious education, and the doormouse. In B. Hyde (Ed.), *The search for a theology of childhood: Essays by Jerome W. Berryman from 1978–2009* (pp. 145–167). Modotti Press.

Bone, J. (2005). Breaking bread: Spirituality, food and early childhood education. *International Journal of Children's Spirituality, 10*(3), 307–317. https://doi.org/10.1080/13644360500347607

Buchanan, M. T. (2021). Identity formation and the role of religious education teachers in Australian Catholic Schools. In R. Wills, M. de Souza, J. Mata-McMahon, M. A. Bakar, & C. Roux (Eds.), *The Bloomsbury handbook of culture and identity from early childhood to early adulthood* (pp. 187–196). Bloomsbury Academic.

Coles, R. (1990). *The spiritual life of children*. Houghton Mifflin Company.

Davids, N. (2021). Muslim-based schools and the risk of enclosing education through socialization in South Africa. In R. Wills, M. de Souza, J. Mata-McMahon, M. A. Bakar, & C. Roux (Eds.), *The Bloomsbury handbook of culture and identity from early childhood to early adulthood* (pp. 93–103). Bloomsbury Academic.

Eaude, T. (2019). The role of culture and traditions in how young children's identities are constructed. *International Journal of Children's Spirituality, 24*(1), 5–19. https://doi.org/10.1080/1364436X.2019.1619534

Eaude, T. (2021). Social and cultural factors and the construction of young children's identities. In R. Wills, M. de Souza, J. Mata-McMahon, M. A. Bakar, & C. Roux (Eds.), *The Bloomsbury handbook of culture and identity from early childhood to early adulthood* (pp. 11–23). Bloomsbury Academic.

Farrugia, R. C. (2021). Learning, potential and identity construction in Maltese early years settings. In R. Wills, M. de Souza, J. Mata-McMahon, M. A. Bakar, & C. Roux (Eds.), *The Bloomsbury handbook of culture and identity from early childhood to early adulthood* (pp. 105–119). Bloomsbury Academic.

Understanding Children's Spirituality in the Literature and Research **41**

Fisher, J. W. (2015). God counts for children's spiritual well-being. *International Journal of Children's Spirituality*, *20*(3–4), 191–203. https://doi.org/10.1080/1364436X.2015.1107033

Frady, K. (2019). Rendering theology with 2-year-old children: A Godly Play and grounded theory combination. *International Journal of Children's Spirituality*, *24*(2), 183–201. https://doi.org/10.1080/1364436X.2019.1619535

Francis, L. J., Fisher, J., Lankshear, D. W., & Eccles, E. L. (2018). Modelling the effect of worship attendance and personal prayer on spiritual well-being among 9-to 11-year-old students attending Anglican church schools in Wales. *International Journal of Children's Spirituality*, *23*(1), 30–44. https://doi.org/10.1080/1364436X.2017.1419938

Goodliff, G. (2013). Spirituality expressed in creative learning: Young children's imagining play as space for mediating their spirituality. *Early Child Development & Care*, *183*(8), 1054–1071. https://doi.org/10.1080/03004430.2013.792253

Gross, Z. (2021). The construction of spiritual identity among Israeli students. In R. Wills, M. de Souza, J. Mata-McMahon, M. A. Bakar, & C. Roux (Eds.), *The Bloomsbury handbook of culture and identity from early childhood to early adulthood* (pp. 301–312). Bloomsbury Academic.

Gulamhusein, S. (2021). Insight into a young Canadian-Muslim's experience of identity. In R. Wills, M. de Souza, J. Mata-McMahon, M. A. Bakar, & C. Roux (Eds.), *The Bloomsbury handbook of culture and identity from early childhood to early adulthood* (pp. 229–238). Bloomsbury Academic.

Gunnestad, A., & Thwala, S. l. (2011). Resilience and religion in children and youth in Southern Africa. *International Journal of Children's Spirituality*, *16*(2), 169–185. https://doi.org/10.1080/1364436X.2011.580726

Harris, K. (2018). The personae of the spiritual child: Taking pictures of the heart using technology and tablets. *International Journal of Children's Spirituality*, *23*(3), 291–305. https://doi.org/10.1080/1364436X.2018.1483324

Hart, L. (2011). Nourishing the authentic self: Teaching with heart and soul. In N. N. Wane, E. L. Manyimo, & E. J. Ritskes (Eds.), *Spirituality, education, and society* (pp. 37–48). Sense Publishers.

Hart, T. (2021). Grounding being in the ground of being: Spiritual experiences as catalysts in identity formation. In R. Wills, M. de Souza, J. Mata-McMahon, M. A. Bakar, & C. Roux (Eds.), *The Bloomsbury handbook of culture and identity from early childhood to early adulthood* (pp. 337–345). Bloomsbury Academic.

Hay, D., & Nye, R. (2006). *The spirit of the child* (Revised ed.). Jessica Kingsley Publishers.

Heidegger, M. (1962). *Being and time* (J. Macquarrie & E. Robinson, Trans.). Harper & Row. (Original work published 1927)

Hlatshwayo, G. M., Muthukrishna, N., & Martin, M. (2018). 'Inhliziyo ekhombisa uthando': Exploring children's conceptions of spirituality. *Journal of Psychology in Africa*, *28*(1), 56–61. https://doi.org/10.1080/14330237.2018.1426809

Holder, M. D., Coleman, B., & Wallace, J. M. (2010). Spirituality, religiousness, and happiness in children aged 8–12 years. *Journal of Happiness Studies*, *11*(2), 131–150. https://doi.org/10.1007/s10902-008-9126-1

Hyde, B. (2008). The identification of four characteristics of children's spirituality in Australian Catholic primary schools. *International Journal of Children's Spirituality*, *13*(2), 117–127. https://doi.org/https://doi.org/10.1080/13644360801965925

42 What Is Children's Spirituality?

Hyde, B. (2018). Pathic knowing, lived sensibility and phenomenological reflections on children's spirituality. *International Journal of Children's Spirituality*, *23*(4), 346–357. https://doi.org/10.1080/1364436X.2018.1526168

Ilisko, D. (2021). Searching for meaning and identity among young people in an uncertain world: Perspectives from Latvia. In R. Wills, M. de Souza, J. Mata-McMahon, M. A. Bakar, & C. Roux (Eds.), *The Bloomsbury handbook of culture and identity from early childhood to early adulthood* (pp. 83–91). Bloomsbury Academic.

James, J. (1997). The talented tenth recalled. In J. James (Ed.), *Transcending the talented tenth.* (pp. 15–34). Routledge.

Katz, Y. (2021). Socialization of identity and culture of Jewish and Arab children and adolescents in Israel. In R. Wills, M. de Souza, J. Mata-McMahon, M. A. Bakar, & C. Roux (Eds.), *The Bloomsbury handbook of culture and identity from early childhood to early adulthood* (pp. 263–273). Bloomsbury Academic.

Keating, N. (2017a). Children's spirituality and the practice of meditation in Irish primary schools. *International Journal of Children's Spirituality*, *22*(1), 49–71. https://doi.org/10.1080/1364436X.2016.1264928

Keating, N. (2017b). How children describe the fruits of meditation. *Religions*, *8*(12), 261. https://doi.org/10.3390/rel8120261

Kilpeläinen, A.-E., & Ruokonen, I. (2018). (Spi)ritual interaction in musical activity for infants in the church space – a qualitative analysis. *International Journal of Children's Spirituality*, *23*(2), 122–135. https://doi.org/10.1080/1364436X.2018.1450734

London, B. (2021). Nurturing a sense of wholeness in children and adolescents from a spiritual perspective. In R. Wills, M. de Souza, J. Mata-McMahon, M. A. Bakar, & C. Roux (Eds.), *The Bloomsbury handbook of culture and identity from early childhood to early adulthood* (pp. 289–300). Bloomsbury Academic.

Lovelock, P., & Adams, K. (2017). From darkness to light: Children speak of divine encounter. *International Journal of Children's Spirituality*, *22*(1), 36–48. https://doi.org/10.1080/1364436X.2016.1268098

Mansour, S. S., & Moloney, R. (2020). Multiple identities: A study of students in an Australian coptic school. *Journal for the Academic Study of Religion*, *33*(1). https://doi.org/10.1558/jasr.36773

Maslow, A. (1970). *Religions, values and peak-experiences.* Viking Press.

Mata, J. (2015). *Spiritual experiences in early childhood education: Four kindergarteners, one classroom.* Routledge.

Mata-McMahon, J. (2016). Reviewing the research in children's spirituality (2005–2015): Proposing a pluricultural approach. *International Journal of Children's Spirituality*, *21*(2), 140–152.

Merleau-Ponty, M. (1962). *Religions, values and peak-experiences* (C. Smith, Trans.). Routledge and Kegan Paul.

Mitchell, M. B., Silver, C. F., & Ross, C. J. (2012). My hero, my friend: Exploring Honduran youths' lived experience of the god-individual relationship. *International Journal of Children's Spirituality*, *17*(2), 137–151. https://doi.org/10.1080/1364436X.2012.721752

Moore, K., Talwar, V., & Bosacki, S. (2012). Canadian children's perceptions of spirituality: Diverse voices. *International Journal of Children's Spirituality*, *17*(3), 217–234. https://doi.org/10.1080/1364436X.2012.742040

Moore, K., Talwar, V., Bosacki, S., & Park-Saltzman, J. (2011). Diverse voices: Children's perceptions of spirituality. *Alberta Journal of Educational Research*, *57*(1), 107–110.

Understanding Children's Spirituality in the Literature and Research   **43**

Moriarty, M. W. (2011). A conceptualization of children's spirituality arising out of recent research. *International Journal of Children's Spirituality*, *16*(3), 271–285.

Mountain, V. (2007). Educational contexts for the development of children's spirituality: Exploring the use of imagination. *International Journal of Children's Spirituality*, *12*(2), 191–205.

Nauli, R. P., & Mulyono, S. (2019). The correlation between spirituality level and emotional resilience in school-aged children in SDN Kayuringin Jaya South Bekasi. *Comprehensive Child & Adolescent Nursing*, *42*, 135–146. https://doi.org/10.1080/2469419 3.2019.1578434

Nortjé, E., & Van der Merwe, L. (2016). Young children and spirituality: Understanding children's connectedness in a group music class. *International Journal of Children's Spirituality*, *21*(1), 3–18. https://doi.org/10.1080/1364436X.2016.1138932

Pandya, S. P. (2017). Effect of a spiritual education programme in developing altruism and prosocial behaviour among children. *International Journal of Children's Spirituality*, *22*(3–4), 220–238. https://doi.org/10.1080/1364436X.2017.1369012

Pettersen, A. (2015). Angels: A bridge to a spiritual pedagogy? *International Journal of Children's Spirituality*, *20*(3–4), 204–217. https://doi.org/10.1080/1364436X.2015.1115233

Pomytkina, L., Moskalyova, L., Podkopaieva, Y., Gurov, S., Podplota, S., & Zlahodukh, V. (2019). Empirical studies of socio-psychological conditions of formation of ideas about the spiritual ideal in primary school children. *International Journal of Children's Spirituality*, *24*(4), 371–388. https://doi.org/10.1080/1364436X.2019.1672626

Priestley, J. (2001). The experience of religious varieties: William James and the postmodern age. In J. Erricker, C. Ota, & C. Erricker (Eds.), *Spiritual education, cultural, religious and social differences: New perspectives for the 21st century* (pp. 184–194). Sussex Academic Press.

Ratcliff, D. (2008). "The spirit of children's past": A century of children's spirituality research. In H. C. Allen (Ed.), *Nurturing children's spirituality: Christian perspectives and best practices* (pp. 21–42). Cascade Books.

Ratcliff, D. (2010). Children's spirituality: Past and future. *Journal of Spiritual Formation & Soul Care*, *3*(1), 6–20.

Rawi, R., & Letchamanan, H. (2021). Mediating culture and identity for Malay and Indian transgender youth in Asia. In R. Wills, M. de Souza, J. Mata-McMahon, M. A. Bakar, & C. Roux (Eds.), *The Bloomsbury handbook of culture and identity from early childhood to early adulthood* (pp. 249–261). Bloomsbury Academic.

Ristiniemi, J., & Ahmadi, F. (2021). Where to and why? Children on meaning and value from a new materiality perspective. *International Journal of Children's Spirituality*, *26*(1–2), 44–66. https://doi.org/10.1080/1364436X.2020.1860913

Robinson, E. (1977). *The original vision: A study of the religious experience of childhood*. Religious Experience Research Unit.

Roux, C., & Becker, A. (2021). The influence of race and religion on identity construction in post-apartheid South Africa. In R. Wills, M. de Souza, J. Mata-McMahon, M. A. Bakar, & C. Roux (Eds.), *The Bloomsbury handbook of culture and identity from early childhood to early adulthood* (pp. 211–227). Bloomsbury Academic.

Sagberg, S. (2008). Children's spirituality with particular reference to a Norwegian context: Some hermeneutical reflections. *International Journal of Children's Spirituality*, *13*(4), 355–370. https://doi.org/10.1080/13644360802439516

Smart, J. J. C. (2022, July 25). Materialism. *Encyclopedia Britannica*. https://www.britannica.com/topic/materialism-philosophy

44 What Is Children's Spirituality?

Steinholt, R. (2007). *'Møte med et kirkerom' og 'Speranzas reise': Rapport fra et teaterprosjekt i Nidarosdomen 2001–2002 ['Children in sacred space' and 'Speranza's journey': Report from a theatre project in the Nidaros Cathedral 2001–2002]*. DMMHs Publikasjonsserie [No. 1/2007].

Stockinger, H. (2019). Developing spirituality – an equal right of every child? *International Journal of Children's Spirituality, 24*(3), 307–319. https://doi.org/10.1080/13644 36X.2019.1646218

Wills, R. (2011). The magic of music: A study into the promotion of children's well-being through singing. *International Journal of Children's Spirituality, 16*(1), 37–46. https://doi.org/10.1080/1364436X.2010.540750

Yeung, G. K. K., & Chow, W.-Y. (2010). 'To take up your own responsibility': The religiosity of Buddhist adolescents in Hong Kong. *International Journal of Children's Spirituality, 15*(1), 5–23.

Yust, K. M. (2003). Toddler spiritual formation and the faith community. *International Journal of Children's Spirituality, 8*(2), 133–149. https://doi.org/10.1080/13644360304626

SECTION II

Spirituality in the Classroom – What Do the Teachers Say?

This section presents the transition from theory and research into practice looking at the classroom from the teachers' perspectives, highlighting their voices, and providing them with opportunities to show us and their early childhood educator colleagues how they understand spirituality, how it informs their practice, and how it can be supported and nurtured in the classroom, particularly within secular settings. Chapter 3 investigates and summarizes research looking into early childhood educators' perceptions of spirituality, what they understand it to be, and how that understanding informs their teaching. Chapter 4 brings us into Ms. Escarfuller's classroom, exploring her understanding of spirituality, and how this has informed her pedagogical approaches. Finally, in Chapter 5, Ms. Escarfuller shares vignettes from her classroom, demonstrating how she supports spirituality for her students through a variety of the content areas she is tasked with teaching, demonstrating how she places spirituality at the heart of her curriculum.

DOI: 10.4324/9781003081463-5

3

LOOKING INTO EARLY CHILDHOOD TEACHERS' PERCEPTIONS OF NURTURING SPIRITUALITY

George was a seven-year-old boy who had to repeat kindergarten due to a health condition that had him out of school for more than half the school year when he was six. He was now in my kindergarten classroom with his younger five-year-old sister who was also one of my students because there was only one class per grade in this recently opened bilingual school. Not surprisingly, not only was he forced to attend class with his younger sister, but he was angry. Angry at being made to repeat a grade, angry at being in the same class as his younger sister, angry at having been ill, angry at me because I was the person "making" him do the schoolwork to "catch-up," angry at having to "catch-up" at all. He was just overall very angry. Needless to say, he manifested his anger in his behavior toward me and his classmates in many ways. He got into fights, acted out during circle time, distracted his peers, and sometimes outright refused to do classwork or homework. To complicate things, this was a dual language program, and he was at a very beginner level of proficiency for the second language being taught.[1] He didn't care about the reasoning behind the classroom rules, he just didn't follow them. I tried it all with George and nothing seemed to work. Talking, explaining, reasoning, mediating, nothing helped me get through to him.

At my wit's end, I resorted to behaviorist approaches for behavior management. I remember reading a book entitled *Positive Discipline* (1996), with a behavior modification approach to behavioral management and implementing some of the strategies recommended to see if they would encourage more positive behavior and deter the focus from being placed on negative behavior. One of those strategies was a sticker-based reward chart, that we filled in at the end of every day, giving stickers to children for their positive behaviors as recognized by their peers. Children would get stickers for helping a friend with their work, for pushing a

DOI: 10.4324/9781003081463-6

48 Spirituality in the Classroom – What Do the Teachers Say?

friend on the swing set, for waiting for a friend to finish and accompany them down the hall, or for waiting patiently for their turn. At the end of the week, we would tally all the stickers and the child with the most of them would receive a diploma for being the most considerate or kindest friend of the week. As you might have guessed, George, was rarely the child with the most stickers. One week in particular, this fact made him so angry that he pulled the chart from the wall, tore it up, and stomped on it, making all the other children furious as well, because now the recognition of their positive acts was destroyed.

This is my favorite anecdote to illustrate the massive failure of behaviorist strategies used to encourage positive behavior in the classroom, and it is not because of the negative behavioral outcome it had, but because George was right, this strategy was all wrong. After I calmed everyone down and was able to talk to him alone, I asked him, "why did you tear it up?" He responded, "because I'm never going to be kindest kid of the week."

He was right, this system was unfair. If I wanted to help him, to encourage him to change his behavior, setting up a competition for positive behavior by comparing him to others who were already well behaved, was not just unfair, but quite idiotic on my part. He needed to be compared to himself, to improve his behavior at his own pace, and not be compared to and competing with the best-behaved children in his class.

I left that chart in the trash and implemented other strategies to recognize the progress of each of my students in a way that worked best for them. I will never forget the lesson in differentiation and equity I received from George, and through the magic of social media, I know for a fact he turned out to be an outstanding young man regardless of my initial failure to help him.

I share this story not to shame my young and inexperienced teacher self, or to be an example of what not to do, or even cast behaviorism in a negative light, but to highlight that when we are fully present with our students when we are able to get quiet enough to recognize what it is that they need from us and listen to what they have to say, we are able to meet them where they are and provide the support they need to improve and shine their brightest light. When we are able to see, truly see, and honor the individual child, we will be in a better place to nurture them spiritually, and once we begin doing that, behavior is bound to change. When children are seen, truly seen for who they are, when adults around them allow for time and space for them to express themselves, their true nature, and recognize them for who they are, children can begin to trust adults, and through this trust build relationships. These nurturing relationships will support the child to continue their development in ways that are aligned with their spirit. When the adult changes their behavior toward the child, the child in turn will change their behavior toward the adult.

Yet in order to intentionally build relationships based on trust and provide spiritual development support for children like George, who might be dealing with a wide variety of issues, teachers need first to be clear on what spirituality is and how they

Looking Into Early Childhood Teachers' Perceptions of Nurturing Spirituality **49**

understand it. Thus, in search of promoting spirituality in educational settings, I set to uncover how early childhood educators understand spirituality, and if they believe it is possible to support and nurture it for their students, even within secular environments.

Research on Educators' Perception on Spirituality

As an early childhood teacher educator and a researcher within the line of inquiry of children's spirituality, I believe part of my role is to support pre-service and in-service educators to learn how to nurture spirituality for children (both individually and collectively); to do that I need to assist them in uncovering what spirituality means to themselves, as I encourage them to embrace the responsibility to foster it for the children they teach. Given this, I set out to understand what teachers think about spirituality and how they nurture it in the classroom. I wanted to know if educators think such 'applied spirituality' is part of their charge as teachers, or if they believe it is solely the families' responsibility. I wanted to know if spiritual development is as important to teachers as it is for me and if so if they have found ways to nurture it in public, secular, educational settings. I wanted to know what they are doing, if anything, to nurture and support children's spirituality. Because of wanting to uncover this knowledge, I have engaged in different projects with in-service and pre-service teachers to shed light on some of these unknowns in the field of children's spirituality. Subsequently, I share some of my work and the work of others in this regard in this chapter.

While I was a doctoral student in New York City, I worked at two separate early childhood centers that allowed me to work closely with early childhood educators from very different backgrounds and levels of trainings. My colleagues came from different countries, were from a variety of races and ethnicities, and worked within different frameworks of belief and disbelief when it came to spirituality. They also ranged in age and years of classroom experience, thus making them a perfect sample for me to explore early childhood educators' understanding of spirituality, and their thoughts regarding it having a place in the classroom as well as being within the teacher's range of responsibilities. I conducted semi-structured interviews with six of my colleagues asking them about their spiritual backgrounds, their understanding of spirituality, and if they believed it was part of their responsibility to nurture it for the children in their classrooms (Mata, 2012).

My findings were interesting, yet unsurprising. The teachers I interviewed either understood spirituality through a religious lens, determined by one's belief in God. Or believed it to be something more universal having innate qualities as it relates to humans and defined it as faith in something that is not of this level, not tangible, that can be felt yet not seen.

The teachers who related spirituality to religion shared that in their view it was illogical to separate God and religion from spirituality. One teacher equated spirituality with morality and explained the sense of right and wrong was not a

50 Spirituality in the Classroom – What Do the Teachers Say?

sociological construct and instead came from somewhere beyond humans, ultimately coming from God, "the one who set up the whole thing" (p. 240). Another teacher with a similar religious understanding of spirituality explained that, even though she knew others might understand the spiritual and the religious as different, she needed the structure provided by monotheistic religion, with scripture and orthodox praxis, to guide herself spiritually.

Conversely, the teachers who understood spirituality as a universal, innately human trait, which allows people to connect with something larger and with one another, stated that it went beyond the notion of God and did not require religion as a guiding structure. They mentioned faith and belief, yet it was not specific to religious dogma, stating, "forget about religion or if you believe in God . . . it's something that just happens because it's part of the human being" (p. 241). Another teacher understood spirituality as a sense of community and being spiritual as responding to the needs of the community one is part of. She shared,

> I would define spirituality as respect for each other, working with each other toward a common goal, whether it's a known goal or unknown, it's almost like a journey together as a community . . . spirituality is having a harmonious relationship with people around us.
>
> *(p. 241)*

A more recent study, looking to examine teachers' perspectives of social-emotional learning and spirituality in public school settings uncovered similar findings regarding teachers' understanding of spirituality. Violante (2022) interviewed 12 kindergarten through twelfth-grade (K-12) public school teachers from Montana and found some teachers understood spirituality in relation to religion, while others understood it in relation to community and self-awareness. These teachers, in the second group, found connections between spirituality and socio-emotional learning, as they explained spirituality can provide a value system that guides students' behavior and overall socio-emotional development. When asked how they supported socio-emotional development and student well-being through spirituality, these teachers shared they would incorporate calming and reflective activities such as moments of silence, breathing exercises, and spending time in nature. Although these teachers recognized various influences on students' spiritual development, including family and cultural background, "they reported that educators also play a role in that development, especially through fostering relationships across diverse backgrounds and varied belief systems" (p. 60).

Later in my career, as a teacher educator working with pre-service teachers, I conducted a study with the students enrolled in one of my teacher education courses (Mata, 2014). Eleven teacher candidates, enrolled in my course, participated in an online discussion on spirituality. I had assigned them two readings, one

Looking Into Early Childhood Teachers' Perceptions of Nurturing Spirituality   **51**

theoretical, a chapter from Tobin Hart's book *The Secret Spiritual World of Children* (2003), and one empirical, the paper summarizing my work with my teacher colleagues while I was in graduate school (Mata, 2012). I also provided a 35-minute presentation on the topic comprising theory and research on children's spirituality. After this exposure, the teacher candidates engaged in an online discussion sharing their thoughts on spirituality and how they understood it; and whether they thought spirituality should be supported in the classroom; if so, they were prompted to provide examples of how they nurtured it among their students. The findings showed some pre-service teachers defined spirituality as being centered around the self, an integral component of themselves, stemming from within. One of them shared,

> spirituality is the relationship between our inner selves, our physical bodies, and our environment. I like to think of the physical body as the bridge that connects our spiritual self with everything around us. . . . I see spirituality more as a philosophy, questioning and examining even your own self, in order to find a place, purpose, and meaning for one's life.
>
> *(p. 116)*

Others understood spirituality as an otherness, as a means to connect with others, nature, the environment, or their immediate surroundings. As one of the pre-service teachers shared,

> my belief is that spirituality includes the connection among human beings and all that surrounds us (nature, animals, thoughts, values, and memories of loved ones who passed away). When we take time to silently think about those deep aspects of life, we get in touch with the spirituality of the universe.
>
> *(p. 117)*

And still others made a point to differentiate their understanding of spirituality from the definition of religion. One teacher candidate explained,

> for me, spirituality is tied to motivation and will. It does not necessarily have anything to do with religion, it is that single entity that gets you going and keeps you going. . . . Spirituality means more than just believing, it's motivating, defining and a relieving feeling that keeps a person uplifted and determined.
>
> *(p. 117)*

And yet, another pre-service teacher explained,

> many people interchange the definition of religion and spirituality when faced with a challenging situation. I know that religion and spirituality have distinct

definitions, but I feel that spirituality is much more difficult to determine. It can be very different depending on the person and their experiences.

(p. 117)

It seems interesting that ten of the 11 teacher candidates defined spirituality as relational and a way to connect with others, as being innately part of being human, and as a means to find meaning in life. And, even if they might have had a religious upbringing, they not only did not define spirituality similarly to religiosity, but they explicitly stated how these concepts were different. Only one of the 11 participants stated she understood spirituality to be religious and lived it through her religious practices. However, I recognize these findings might have been due to the fact the pre-service teachers had all completed readings and had participated in the lecture on spirituality before sharing their definitions and understandings on the discussion forum.

A few years later, I had the opportunity to again introduce spirituality in a seminar I taught to pre-service early childhood educators. They were also asked to complete readings on spirituality and had several class sessions that dove into the topic from theoretical, conceptual, and empirical perspectives.[2] At the beginning of the seminar, I asked my students to share what spirituality means to them, inviting them to engage in an exercise of reexamining their roots related to spirituality and finding their definitions to share with the class. These students' definitions included a focus on the other, defining spirituality as community; a focus on stages of life and states of mind, defining spirituality as new beginnings, as promoting peace, patience, and calmness; and defining spirituality as a source of happiness and positivity, highlighting the positive aspects of spirituality. These students' definitions can be seen in Figures 3.1, and 3.2. Others in this course had a broader understanding of spirituality, defining it as more than just the person or their relation to others, going beyond the individual yet including them. These definitions can be observed in Figures 3.3 and 3.4.

In a different section of this ECE seminar, conducted during the COVID-19 pandemic, students had a more personal focus when defining spirituality, and as our class sessions were conducted online, they seemed to prefer the use of words more than illustrations to portray and share their definitions. Below, in Figures 3.5 and 3.6, are two definitions centered around how spirituality impacts the self as it relates to nature and to the body, defined through poems.

Findings from this course redesign experience are further explored in Chapter 7, where I explain how through daily meditation practices and mindfulness projects and assignments, teacher preparation programs can support early childhood education teacher candidates in exploring spirituality, and how it can be nurtured for young children in secular settings.

In a survey study I conducted with my colleagues Michael Haslip and Deborah Schein (Mata-McMahon et al., 2020), we asked 33 early childhood educators

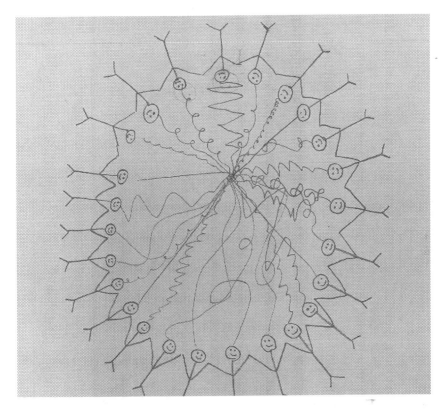

FIGURE 3.1 Spirituality as community (Vicky, September 11, 2019)

Source: Jennifer Mata-McMahon

working in secular educational settings with children ages between birth and eight, how they understood spirituality.[3] The educators who participated as respondents of the survey were mainly female (n=31), majorly white (n=24), mainly general educators (n=14), with ten or more years of experience (n=25), primarily worked with preschoolers (n=22), worked mainly in private secular settings (n=22), in urban regions (n=17), representing 16 different states in the U.S. After qualitative grounded theory analysis, to uncover codes and themes, the findings showed eight salient concepts stemming from the educators' answer to the question, "What do you understand children's spirituality to be?" They defined these concepts as:

a. promoting connections (to others, with nature, and to the universe at large);
b. practicing values (including love, forgiveness, compassion, respect, care, kindness, empathy, etc.);

FIGURE 3.2 Spirituality as happiness and positivity (Ginger, September 11, 2019)
Source: Jennifer Mata-McMahon

c. making meaning (through curiosity, questioning, and accepting other's ideas and beliefs);
d. relating to God and religious practices (through mentions of God, the Bible, angels, soul, spirit, and Jesus);
e. self-awareness;
f. mindfulness and presence;

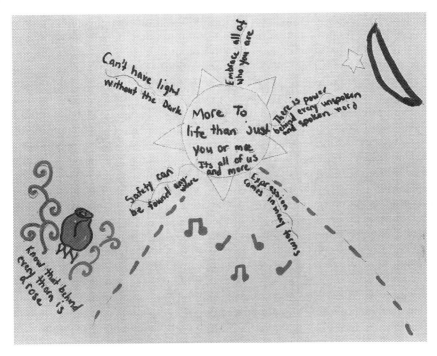

FIGURE 3.3 Spirituality as all of us and more (Megan, September 11, 2019)

Source: Jennifer Mata-McMahon

g. humaneness; and
h. inner feelings as ways in which they understood and defined spirituality.

In looking at how early childhood educators understand spirituality within different educational settings, frameworks, and countries, I found a few studies conducted abroad that are worth mentioning as they help us deepen and broaden our knowledge base. Kaili Chen Zhang (2014), explored early childhood education teachers', principals', and parents' perceptions of the role of spirituality in the lives of children with special needs and how educators and schools support spiritual development. Zhang purposefully selected three preschools each with an educational philosophy that includes the spiritual, and thus these sites implemented faith-based curricula or included spirituality in their pedagogical approach. The sites studied were a Buddhist, a Christian, and a Waldorf school in Hong Kong. Zhang found that both parents and educators explained spirituality as helping children to enjoy and appreciate life, affecting children's emotional and physical well-being, and self-determination. They spoke of spirituality as supporting relationship building, promoting connectedness with the self and others, encouraging wonder and understanding of the world around

56 Spirituality in the Classroom – What Do the Teachers Say?

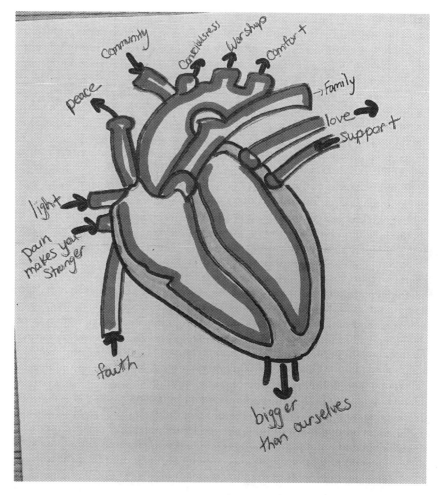

FIGURE 3.4 Spirituality as bigger than ourselves (Mindy, September 11, 2019)

Source: Jennifer Mata-McMahon

us, and appreciating others. Principals in these schools spoke of the focus being placed on "helping children to discover joy, meaning, purpose, and values in life" (p. 1738). Admittedly, this study had a small sample size (N=24) and was carried out in faith-based schools, that arguably are founded on the basis of recognizing the value and importance of spirituality in human development, yet the findings coincide with what teachers and educators are saying about spirituality across different contexts.

In New Zealand, stemming from the *Te Whāriki Curriculum's* vision statement, which highlights the responsibility teachers have to create environments in which

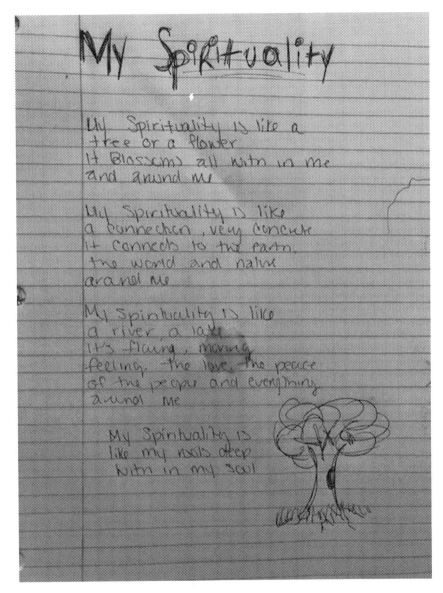

FIGURE 3.5 Spirituality as related to nature (Kelly, September 19, 2020)

Source: Jennifer Mata-McMahon

children can develop holistically, including developing spiritually, Cheryl Faye Greenfield (2018) conducted a small qualitative study looking into "teachers' perspectives on their understanding of spirituality and 'wairua'[4] and the role they have in fostering these aspects in children's development" (p. 275). Greenfield surveyed

58   Spirituality in the Classroom – What Do the Teachers Say?

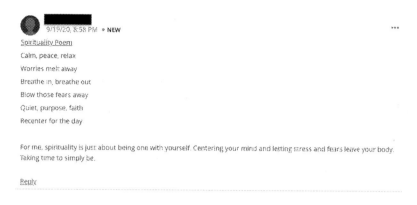

FIGURE 3.6   Spirituality in the body (Tammy, September 19, 2020)

Source: Jennifer Mata-McMahon

24 early childhood in-service teachers asking them about their understanding of and views on:

> *wairua*; spirituality; what they understood the identified statements in *Te Whāriki* to mean for them in practice as a teacher; how intentional their fostering of spirituality and *wairua* were; what role the physical environment plays in nurture [*sic*] a child's spirit; whether their initial teacher education programme covered fostering spirituality; and how they would benefit from participating in professional development on the topic.
>
> (p. 281)

Greenfield found that respondents thought *wairua* was about the spirit, soul, inner being, heart, the sum of who we are, and the core of the person. Several respondents mentioned that they thought *wairua* can be passed on through generations between people, places, and things. Some commented that one's *wairua* must be nurtured, protected, and cared for. Others described one's *wairua* as the part of the self that motivates outward actions and is part of one's personality. Two teachers mentioned that *wairua* is about being connected to God. Yet, most insisted it is something to be nurtured and cared for since people's *wairua* or lack thereof can affect relationships and the environment.[5]

Spirituality was similarly described by these teachers. They thought spirituality was about the soul and the essence that defines us, about who we are, as was their understanding of *wairua*. Spirituality was seen as an aspect of humankind that seeks justice, celebrates diversity, and is creative. Some participants referred to spirituality as inner joy, peace, and happiness, while others mentioned aspects like consciousness, something you feel, a connectedness to others, God, and the environment. Eight participants made a point of differentiating spirituality from

Looking Into Early Childhood Teachers' Perceptions of Nurturing Spirituality   59

religion, explaining that spirituality was about belief in a higher power or God, without the necessity of that belief being bound by the structure provided by religion. Overall, these teachers thought spirituality was the part that makes us who we are and the energy inside us that connects us to things that are of importance to us; they explained it is not tactile, yet it can be felt as it connects us to the broader environment.

This Australian study is very interesting as it reflects teachers who work with the Maori population seem to have a very similar understanding of spirituality as they do of *wairua*. These definitions closely relate to what previously studied pre-service and in-service teachers from different cultural backgrounds and geographical locations have to say regarding spirituality. When asked about their role in supporting children's spirituality, most of the teachers agreed that it is part of their responsibility as they support the holistic development of children, by caring, protecting, and respecting each child. When asked how they intentionally support spirituality for their students, teachers reported: through *karakia*[6] and prayer, respectful relationships, learning *whakapapa*,[7] providing an environment where children can express themselves and talk about what is important to them, among other ways to listen, care, and connect.

These teachers thought the environment played a salient role in helping them provide support for children's spiritual development. They mentioned needing the environment to be clean, aesthetically pleasing, safe, not too crowded, and able to allow children to move at their own pace. They also mentioned providing non-fiction books and having culturally responsive resources reflecting children's own backgrounds as well as having sensory-appropriate colors and lighting. Most all teachers indicated that providing an inviting, stress-free, peaceful, engaging environment filled with natural resources and nature was optimal for supporting children's spiritual development.

Another qualitative study conducted in Australia by Christine Robinson (2019) looked into the mandated early childhood framework requiring educators working in early childhood services to attend to children's spirituality. Particularly, she focused on the component of this framework tasking educators with promoting children's connectedness with and contribution to the world, including the natural environment. Robinson interviewed and observed nine early childhood educators, across eight classrooms, within three centers, working with children between three and four years of age, to determine their understandings and practices around promoting children's spirituality in the context of religious childcare centers in Western Australia, aligned with a focus on nature engagement. Robinson found that teachers were well-versed in articulating the connection between spirituality and engagement with nature in childhood.

However, in practice, educators rarely offered opportunities for children to experience nature. When defining spirituality, the educators explained they found "nature really spiritual" (Robinson, 2019, p. 345), and as being connected to

60 Spirituality in the Classroom – What Do the Teachers Say?

feeling at peace which was associated with natural environments. The teachers explained that children expressed spirituality through their connections with people and the natural environment, and they recognized the need to provide time for children to be engaged with and to develop a personal relationship with nature as a practice for promoting spirituality, which seems consistent with what previously studied educators mentioned while defining spirituality (Schein, 2012). Observational data showed in all three centers, opportunities for outdoor play were made available for children, yet even though educators provided the context for engagement with the natural world, they did not facilitate, nor did they provide added value to children's experience with the natural environment. It seemed evident that educators emphasized relational experiences with human others rather than relational opportunities for children with the natural world, to support children spiritually.

Gillespie (2019) conducted a qualitative study in Kent in the U.K., with five primary school teachers who had a minimum of five years' teaching experience, looking into their understanding of spirituality and how this related to their professional practices. Semi-structured interviews were used to collect the data that was then analyzed using an interpretive phenomenological analysis (IAP) method (Eatough & Smith, 2007; Willig, 2009). These teachers understood spirituality as moments of connection and profundity which then led them to change. Teachers "sought to facilitate individuals' reflecting on their identity and agency by providing the tools to seek out and question for themselves elements of social action" (p. 333). The teachers shared that for them education is not just for the learning of areas within the curriculum but through positive relationships, education should provide pupils and colleagues with the tools they need to become active participants in society and where possible seek change. They proposed this change started with the self and reported that when they were able to guide others to see themselves in certain ways would not only improve their concept of self and self-esteem but possibly assist in personal and social change. Teachers also demonstrated and recognized that they leveraged their spiritual beliefs and frameworks to make sense of and challenge assumed understandings in difficult social interactions with children and families; in this sense spirituality was closely aligned with what teachers understood as their professional role. They understood "the educational process as an expression of the interaction between their professional identity and their spirituality" (p. 337).

Similarly, to Australia, Canada, and the U.K., the Chilean General Law of Education states that one of the purposes of education is the spiritual development of all its schooled population. Through semi-structured interviews, Vargas-Herrera and Moya-Marchant (2018) studied 20 principals from secular and religious schools, to determine their understanding of students' spiritual development. Findings showed that school principals understood spirituality to be a typical

Looking Into Early Childhood Teachers' Perceptions of Nurturing Spirituality **61**

human ability that can be strengthened in schools, and they believe spirituality is highly important and needs to be intentionally addressed in school settings. They also mentioned seeing a strong relation between spiritual development and ethical and moral development. Even though there were some differences among secular and religious school principals, all study participants seemed to believe spiritual development to be a part of holistic and high-quality education and thus imperative to be addressed for their students.

In summary, from reviewing these studies we find common threads among educators' perceptions of spirituality and how they conceptualize and define it. Key findings presented in this chapter show us that it is typical to find teachers who have a religious understanding of spirituality and define and experience it through the structure provided by religious faith and practices. Yet, we also find an abundance of educators who understand spirituality as innately human, part of the core of human beings, and thus a universal ability; one that is not tangible, that involves faith and beliefs, yet can be unrelated to religious dogma. These educators understand spirituality as self-awareness, centered around the self, and also as a way to connect and relate to others, to their community, and to nature. They relate spirituality with an expression of values such as peace, patience, happiness, and positivity. Spirituality seems to provide them with a sense of calmness and through experiences of wonder promotes meaning-making. As well, directors and school principals seem to agree on the importance of spirituality as a typical ability, innately human, as they related it to ethical and moral development, and thus saw it as central to a school's mission to nurture it. They also spoke of values, joy, meaning-making, and purpose as aspects facilitated through spirituality.

When asked how spirituality can be supported in the classroom, teachers across all of these studies mentioned calming and reflective activities such as moments of silence, breathing exercises, and being in nature. They also highlighted the nurturing relationships teachers can promote by listening, protecting, respecting, caring for, and connecting with children. The classroom environment was also mentioned as a key component in supporting the spiritual development of children. When speaking of the classroom, teachers mentioned that providing a clean, calm, aesthetically pleasing, safe, and orderly environment was important. They also spoke of materials that were culturally responsive and environments that had sensory-appropriate colors and lighting.

Taken together, the summary of key findings presented earlier illustrates the commonalities found across these studies regarding how early childhood educators understand spirituality, even when crossing cultural and geographical borders around the world. In the following chapters, Ms. Escarfuller introduces us to her own understanding of spirituality and how it has informed her pedagogy both in the ways she teaches the mandated district and state curricula and in how she supports and nurtures spirituality for her students.

62 Spirituality in the Classroom – What Do the Teachers Say?

Notes

1. I had been trained as a constructivist early childhood educator, and as such was used to managing behavior through facilitating and mediating an understanding of the usefulness of classroom rules. For example, we walk in the classroom because we want to avoid getting hurt or hurting others, we take turns to speak because we want to be able to listen to others, and we share our materials because working together and leveraging our strengths helps us build friendships and generate better projects.
2. The design of this seminar is explained in detail in Chapter 7.
3. This survey has been validated as an instrument entitled "Early Childhood Educators' Spiritual Practices in the Classroom (ECE-SPC)" (Mata-McMahon et al., under review), and will be used in a wider national study to determine how educators across the U.S. understand spirituality and how they are nurturing it in their settings. It is my hope the findings collected through this instrument will contribute to add and deepen our understanding of how spirituality is defined by educators and is being addressed in classrooms across the country.
4. Tihei Mauri Ora – Behold there is Life! Māori believe the sneeze of life, the mauri, was breathed into the body and created humankind. The combination of the physical body and the mauri created the wairua – a living soul. While mauri is the intrinsic power that brings life, wairua allows us to relate to others. We are all born with taha tinana (our body), taha hinengaro (our mind), and taha wairua (our spirit); these are integral to shaping every person. Taha wairua relates to the unseen and unspoken energies. For some people, wairua (spirituality) is about having faith and religious practices, for others it's an internal connection to the universe or the sacred (Defense Health Hub, 2022).
5. They explained places have a *wairua* as well.
6. Karakia are *prayers* or *incantations*. They are generally used to ensure a favorable outcome to important events and undertakings such as tangihanga (*the ritual of farewell to our deceased*), hui (*meetings*), and unveilings; however, they can cover every aspect of life. For example: welcoming the dawn and farewelling the day, to ensure a safe journey, for different types of illness, when undertaking tā moko (*tribal 'tatoo'*), when carving wharenui (*meeting houses*) or waka (*traditional canoe*), and more. Karakia, in their true essence, are ritual chants invoking spiritual guidance and protection (University of Otago, 2022a).
7. While whakapapa is about the recitation of genealogy – lineage or ancestry – it also literally means to 'place in layers' or 'create a base'. It places our people in a wider context, linking us to a common ancestor, our ancestral land, our waterways, and our tribal (and sub-tribal) groupings. Hence, the literal translation fits with the broader meaning of ancestry and the expansive nature of its 'layers' (University of Otago, 2022b).

References

Defense Health Hub. (2022). *What is Wairua?* Defense Force. Retrieved September 19, 2022, from https://health.nzdf.mil.nz/your-health/soul/what-is-wairua/

Eatough, V., & Smith, J. A. (2007). Interpretive phenomenological analysis. In E. Lyons & A. Coyle (Eds.), *Analysing qualitative data in psychology* (pp. 35–50). SAGE.

Gillespie, A. (2019). Teachers' spirituality as an element of social action. An interpretative phenomenological analysis of primary teachers' understanding and expression of spirituality. *International Journal of Children's Spirituality, 24*(4), 328–340. https://doi.org/10.1080/1364436X.2019.1684880

Greenfield, C. F. (2018). Investigation into New Zealand early childhood teachers' perspectives on spirituality and Wairua in teaching. *International Journal of Children's Spirituality, 23*(3), 275–290. https://doi.org/10.1080/1364436X.2018.1460333

Hart, T. (2003). *The secret spiritual world of children*. Inner Ocean Publishing.

Mata, J. (2012). Nurturing spirituality in early childhood classrooms: The teacher's view. In M. Fowler, J. D. Martin, & J. L. Hochheimer (Eds.), *Spirituality: Theory, praxis and pedagogy* (pp. 239–248). Inter-Disciplinary Press.

Mata, J. (2014). Sharing my journey and opening spaces: Spirituality in the classroom. *International Journal of Children's Spirituality, 19*(2), 112–122. https://doi.org/10.1080/1364436X.2014.922464

Mata-McMahon, J., Haslip, M. J., & Kruse, L. (under review). Validation study of the Early Childhood Educators' Spiritual Practices in the Classroom (ECE-SPC) instrument using rasch. *International Journal of Children's Spirituality*.

Mata-McMahon, J., Haslip, M. J., & Schein, D. L. (2020). Connections, virtues, and meaning-making: How early childhood educators describe children's spirituality. *Early Childhood Education Journal, 48*(5), 657–669. https://doi.org/10.1007/s10643-020-01026-8

Robinson, C. (2019). Young children's spirituality: A focus on engaging with nature. *Australasian Journal of Early Childhood, 44*(4), 339–350. https://doi.org/10.1177/1836939119870907

Schein, D. (2012). *Early childhood educators' perceptions of spiritual development in young children: A social constructivist grounded theory study* [Doctoral Dissertation, Walden University].

University of Otago. (2022a). *Karakia – Prayers*. University of Otago. Retrieved September 19, 2022, from www.otago.ac.nz/maori/world/te-reo-maori/karakia-prayers/index.html

University of Otago. (2022b). *Mihi – Introductions*. University of Otago. Retrieved September 19, 2022, from www.otago.ac.nz/maori/world/te-reo-maori/mihi-introductions/index.html

Vargas-Herrera, F., & Moya-Marchant, L. (2018). Spiritual development: Understanding and importance in schools: An analysis based on statements made by school directors from Valparaíso, Chile. *International Journal of Children's Spirituality, 23*(3), 323–336. https://doi.org/10.1080/1364436X.2018.1488680

Violante, A. E. (2022). *A qualitative examination of teacher's perspectives of social-emotional learning and spirituality in the public school setting* [(Publication Number 11890) Graduate Student Theses, Dissertations, & Professional Papers, University of Montana].

Willig, C. (2009). *Introducing qualitative research in psychology*. Open University Press.

Zhang, K. C. (2014). Through a spiritual lens: Early childhood inclusive education in Hong Kong. *Journal of Religion and Health, 53*(6), 1728–1740. https://doi.org/10.1007/s10943-013-9771-5

4

HOW MS. ESCARFULLER'S SPIRITUALITY INFORMS HER PEDAGOGY

In opening this chapter, I invite you into the delicate ironic work of being an educator, a leader, and a positive role model to other people's children (while I at times struggle to be that at home with my own children). I empathize with the parent who confides in me that her child triggers her in a way that makes her identify with Dr. Jekyll and Mr. Hyde. I know we are all doing our best, given what we know and what we carry. We all wake up to face challenges and the opportunity for spiritual growth available in each of these challenges; there is never a dull moment. I know we are learning from each other; we are learning from our children how to be more loving and harmonious within ourselves and with others. I know that theory is easier than practice. Still, I choose every day to nurture my own spirituality and spiritual growth to serve children better so they may exist more harmoniously with themselves and with others, as I strive to do.

Defining Spirituality

So, what is spirituality for me? To get myself to give a publicly printed definition of spirituality required much introspection, procrastination, and release of fear; fear that I have it all wrong. After all, volumes have been written on the subject, and still, it seems an elusive concept to me. I imagine that I am only glancing at a piece of spirituality as I aim to define it. As it is, my spirituality does inform my pedagogy and therefore how I see and choose to nurture children's spirituality in the classroom.

My own definition of spirituality remains like an ocean in constant motion and evolution. At times, I have seen spirituality as a noun, as the essence of our humanness. At times, I have seen spirituality as a verb, an action being taken toward finding meaning in life. Today, at this moment, I see spirituality as both a

DOI: 10.4324/9781003081463-7

How Ms. Escarfuller's Spirituality Informs Her Pedagogy **65**

noun and a verb. My spirituality is at once the essence of my being and the experience of being spirit embodied in human form. To separate spirituality from the essence of who I am is akin to separating breath from the human experience – you cannot experience humanity without it. I am like a fish swimming in the ocean of spirit, filled by it, alive in it, and acting with it.

To me, spirituality means making meaning. It means understanding the purpose of human existence and all of existence. It means understanding the experience of being human and the interconnectedness of all life. Spirituality is holding reverence and love for all experiences.

Therefore, spirituality is also acting in accordance with our Highest Self, our Spirit or Soulful Self. From this Highest Self, we act with the authentic power of responding to a situation instead of reacting to a situation. When in line with our Highest Self, we respond from a place of secure worth and wholeness. We embrace all ranges of emotion, thought, sensation, and life circumstances with a suffering-free stance, an acceptance of our reality just as it is. Our heart remains open and accepting. We can create space between the situation and how we reply to it. When we react, we are coming from a place of fear and insecurity. We are acting from a protective stance. Our heart constricts and rejects the experience. We have a 'trigger' go off and then our thoughts, emotions, and sensations take over; an urge rises to fix or reject the situation. Spirituality is the practice of staying in alignment with our Highest Self so that we accept all as it is and choose actions that create harmony instead of harm. Therefore, the goal of spirituality is to lead the fullest potential of our existence in harmony with all of Creation.

Spirituality aims to exercise all aspects of our humanity to work in unison with Spirit to respond to our world from that state of inner unity. Achieving this inner unity requires being a vigilant observer of self from within and from the outside and gives us the power to nurture and feed loving action. So, for me it thus follows, that to nurture spirituality to its fullest one must have an awareness of the laws governing Spirit, and as such the laws of the Universe.

> Bridging the gap between spirituality and science, Albert Einstein wrote, "A spirit is involved in the Laws of the Universe" – a spirit vastly superior to that of man, and one in the face of which we, with our modest powers, must feel humble.
>
> *(Wolf, 1996, p. 10)*

As an educator, I bear a weighty responsibility to model these truths and to reveal the wonder of the Universe to the children, so they may create in our world from their Highest Self. Sofia Cavalletti wrote:

> As Montessorians, I think, we contradict ourselves if we do not satisfy the child's thirst for the transcendent, his most basic need. We prevent the method

66 Spirituality in the Classroom – What Do the Teachers Say?

from fully attaining its aim: the harmonious living of people. The Montessori Method . . . [by] its very nature is spiritual, and we violate its nature if we deprive it of its full spiritual blossoming.

(1978, p. 14)

My role is to guide the children in my care to know their worth and potential impact on this universe through their actions, so that they may wisely choose their actions and creations. I also bear the duty to nurture my own spirituality, preparing myself as an adult, to live up to this aspiration.

Past the pile of papers yet to be graded, the display of children's proudly completed work, and the myriad of curricular work in progress, may a visitor also observe a child waking up to his/her inner drive and Highest Self. That through the children's intellectual activity, an observer may glimpse the children's subtle spiritual work guiding their social, emotional, and sensorial aspects of their beings. Imagine what our world would be like if we focused on exercising these aspects from an early age to the same degree as mental development. In the words of Dr. Maria Montessori, "Society must recognize the importance of the child as the builder of humanity and come to have a profound appreciation for the psychic roots determining whether the mature adult will seek positive or negative goals" (Montessori, 2015, p. 34).

So how did I get here? Like you, my environment, education, culture, faith, relationships, and life experiences have all shaped my definition of spirituality and my path in work. In all of that, there are key experiences that shaped my own sense of spirituality. These moments fit into three categories. The first category includes 'supernatural' childhood experiences that no one around me at that time could explain and which I eventually refrained from sharing because I was terrified of being rejected. At the same time, these experiences gave me some sense of who I was in the world; in nature, I understood my place and felt a deep connection to something intangible at the time.

The second category constitutes my religious-based experiences and my formation of faith. My third-grade teacher Sister Margaritis, at St Francis of Assisi School in New Orleans, shaped my belief in miracles, divine protection, and faith that 'God has a special plan' and purpose for every one of us; just a year earlier I had moved to New Orleans as a Dominican immigrant, entering a land of foreign language, people, and environment and my Catholic faith gave me much-needed safety and security. This faith foundation tethered me through all sorts of life experiences and filled me with hope. The saints were my models here.

The third category includes the natural human suffering I experienced, as we all do, and my innate desire to live life in a way that minimized suffering to myself or to others. I wanted to be a hero, like the saints, bearing all circumstances with equanimity and acceptance. How wonderful to achieve a state of constant joyous miracles.

How Ms. Escarfuller's Spirituality Informs Her Pedagogy   **67**

My first memory of sensing a deep connection to the intangible or 'supernatural' started at the age of five. One morning, I walked through Santo Domingo's outdoor market compelled by the smells of fresh coal-roasted peanuts, the bright colors, the cool sweetness of *menta verde*, and the rhythmic joyous sounds of merengue intertwined with people's voices. As I passed the chicken vendor, my eyes met the eyes of one of his chickens and I knew that chicken would be selected next for slaughter. So, I spoke to the chicken, like one would an imaginary friend, wishing the chicken well, that she may go peacefully, that she was very beautiful, and that I loved her. Indeed, she was selected for sale next, and I still remember standing stunned and wondering at the magic of the moment. I wondered, could I predict accurately again? I could. I decided to keep this superpower as my secret and the chickens became my 'imaginary friends'. I had made an indelible connection. Compelled by my experiences, I continued to visit the outdoor market near the chicken seller, situating myself on a wooden crate where I could see all the transactions of the chicken vendor. As I unknowingly practiced developing this sense, I continued to see 'in my mind' other events before they happened, both sad and joyous. These unexplainable events solidified that something else was at work beyond what I was learning at home or school. My questioning nature, curiosity, and openness to all things different and beyond the ordinary were cemented.

This leads me into my second category of my religious formation and Catholic elementary education. In the summer of 1977, I moved permanently to the U.S. to live with my father. That fall, I entered second grade to discover that I was the only one who did not speak English; no one understood Spanish either. A year later, having learned to protect myself with juicy American curse words, I found myself having recess indoors with my third-grade teacher Sister Margaritis; she is the reason I became a teacher. With this special recess time with her, I quickly improved my English speaking, writing, and reading and had my multiplication tables down weeks before the other children. This time in my teacher's classroom held wonder, peace, calm, and joy. I felt confident and successful there. I began to spend time in the nunnery after school and I learned more about the miracles of Jesus and the lives of saints who could pardon even the most heinous crimes done to them. Mind-boggling! Jesus' and the saints' lives entranced and inspired me with all the magic and miracles; they could transform suffering into joy and love! As an elementary child, I was engrossed by the books recounting the miracles performed and adventures lived of these real-life heroes. How could they stay so loving in the face of massive adversity? How could I manifest a life of miracles and magic? What if we all knew how?

At some point, I became interested in the internal life of Jesus and that led me to discover Buddhism. Achieving a Highest Self state, and staying in loving action, seemed attainable through several practices such as meditation and mindfulness. Just like in my Catholic faith, there was a path for directing my words, thoughts, and actions, free of judgment. Almost simultaneously, I developed a

68   Spirituality in the Classroom – What Do the Teachers Say?

friendship with an older couple who seemed kindred in spirit. They had traveled around the world, he as a photojournalist and she as a writer, mom, and publisher. Their home was filled with rich simplicity. Our conversations wondered about the beauty of nature and stewardship of its beauty. We talked about current issues of justice, here at home and abroad. We shared much in common about seeing the light in everyone, and the love in all things. Through them, I discovered the Quaker way of life. Today, the Buddhist practice of centering and the Quaker way of life continue to guide the direction of my spirituality.

My third category is of human suffering. As a child, I lived in the 'right' neighborhood, attending a 'good' school and mingling with 'successful' families. I remember the Sunday brunches after Catholic Mass near the Mississippi River embraced by the upbeat jazz, attending musicals, operas, and the Nutcracker Ballet at Christmas. Summers from 11 years of age forward, I enjoyed travel back to the Dominican Republic where I stepped into a land of trusted friends with whom I spent summer days and evenings worshipping in Church, attending movies, swimming at the beaches, dancing, and strolling along the *Malecón*. Everything had joy and a sense of adventure.

Amid that, I felt terrified to share my feelings, thoughts, interests, and abilities. So, I tried to please everyone around me to feel safe and worthy. Perfection would have made a good middle name for me at that time. I meticulously found ways to improve my environment, my work, myself, and others (not so well received). I did not dare to disclose my feelings of shame, guilt, anger, sadness, judgment, or fear. These feelings were wrong in my mind, and I would fix them. I would fix these feelings and never suffer.

Eventually, I became an adult and went into teaching inspired by Sr. Margaritis who seemed to only be made of limitless wonder, patience, gratefulness, and contentment. I loved the idea of studying to fix, improve, and expand myself and others; teaching seemed a perfect match for me. I graduated from the University of Minnesota with a traditional teacher certification in Art, K-12.

A few years later, I became a parent; this was transformative. When I had my firstborn, a fervent love for him put my perfectionism into overdrive to work on me, on him, and everything surrounding him so he could have an extraordinary life. What did it take to stay in confident loving presence, in joyful gratitude for oneself, others, and our world? How do I raise another soul to be his Highest Self? So, I did what I knew. I studied. Given what I knew then, I could not have predicted where my perfectionism was going to take me; it was not pretty. I was not aligned with my Highest Self. I learned through friction, and I regret I did not have then the skills I have now.

I studied some more. I trained in the Community Conferencing circle process, adapted from Australia, by Lauren Abramson, for conflict resolution. I attended trainings around Non-Violent Communication founded by Marshall B. Rosenberg. I read books and articles by Pema Chödrön and Thich Nhat Hanh.

I attended a workshop retreat on an organic farm to learn about manifesting through Conscious Language from Faith Bost. I also learned about the new findings in quantum physics proving that we are energy, in *The Quantum Enigma* by Bruce Rosenblum and Fred Kuttner. I read the *Biology of Belief* by Bruce Lipton. I took a Conscious Parenting Revolution course, founded and taught by Katherine Winter-Sellery. I read about nutrition and somatics. I was determined as today to find every angle possible to align all aspects of myself to achieve a state of inner harmony, of my spiritual best. And I still study. I also continue to learn through the 'friction' of life experiences.

The most formative aspect for me as an educator, however, has been completing training and graduating in 2019 as an AMI Montessori Elementary Guide for ages 6–12, along with my work in the Montessori classroom both as an assistant and as a guide. Here I found an educational roadmap weaving all aspects of what it means to be human and how to nurture another soul to be his/her best self. Simultaneously, I found a guide to nurture myself to be the best version of me for the children. In the Montessori method of education, I could, as required, focus my attention foremost on nurturing, not hindering, the spirit of another human being while preparing them to be their best and fullest.

How Spirituality Informs Pedagogy

Having given you a brief history of how I have formed my definition of spirituality and why it matters to me, I now share some of my beliefs that inform my pedagogy:

1. we are inherently perfect;
2. everyone comes here to serve a unique purpose;
3. everything that happens serves and favors us;
4. we are spiritual beings having spiritual experiences through the body, heart, and mind;
5. we are energy;
6. we are manifesters;
7. children are full human beings;
8. a child's thoughts, emotions, and needs matter, and equally as an adult's;
9. every behavior aims to meet a need; and
10. everyone evolves, shifts, and grows.

Perfection

Believing we are inherently perfect means we make zero mistakes. Therefore, everything that happens is serving our highest good. With my heart, I believe it's all in our favor and all perfect. My mind still wonders about this truth.

70 Spirituality in the Classroom – What Do the Teachers Say?

When someone cuts me off in traffic, or I suffer the loss of a relative to Alzheimer's, or I see another news story about injustice, I wonder how everything is still perfect, whole, and complete.

Perhaps everything is perfect because it all creates an opportunity to realign our humanity with our spirit. For every action we take, there is an equal and opposite reaction that reflects our alignment with spirit; you reap what you sow. I then see our reactions to be a self-correcting feedback loop. From my readings thus far, I understand that the feedback loop will eventually align the body, mind, and heart with spirit. We will feel friction in our lives until we accept the truth given to us by the feedback loop. So, the process of self-perfecting to act from the Highest Self, one with Source is perfection itself. In sum, I have the option to accept whatever presents itself or I can resist what has happened. I understand that everything is Spirit's way of communicating to me some truth. This then implies that what I experience in the classroom is perfect as it is because it signals some growth, some will of Spirit, for of each of the children's spirit, as well as my own.

With this belief, the need arises to make the classroom a judgment-free zone. As Katherine Winter-Sellery mentions in her Conscious Parenting Revolution course, we create a 'No Guilt No Blame No Fault No Shame Zone'. When I create this judgment-free zone, I see a child transform as if by magic. I recall Hydon, eight years old, who arrived at my classroom quietly crying and whimpering that he did not get to be line leader today. Even after identifying and acknowledging his disappointment and empathizing with his disappointment, he seemed to have no relief. He instead went to the back of the classroom and began to knock down with his right hand a stack of nine-inch round storage containers. There were a total of 50. Since none of the children seemed disturbed by this or distracted from their work, I proceeded with my lesson as I kept one eye on him. Once I completed my lesson and the children were working independently, I approached him again. He reiterated, "I did not get to be line leader! I will never be line leader!" I again expressed my understanding and extended my empathy. How awful it might feel to not be included. He looked up and said, "Yeah." He went to leave the area, walking through the containers strewn on the floor. I invited him to put the containers back in their place (I dreaded what might come next: resistance!). He stated it was too much to clean up. I stated I would be with him and had faith he could do this 'big job'. He sat on the floor and crossed his arms. I walked away to attend to the other children. At the end of class, he had not picked up the containers. I asked the other teacher for assistance in walking the class back to their homeroom. Hydon started crying that he would be left behind. I reminded him that his class would be there for him when he was ready, that everyone had cleaned up after themselves – we were being fair. I would be there to support his work, and I would give him all the time he needed so he could have the ability to say, "I did it!" I said enthusiastically. Twenty minutes later, Hydon had cleaned up his work. "Congratulations! You did it!" "I did it!" he exclaimed. I walked with

How Ms. Escarfuller's Spirituality Informs Her Pedagogy **71**

him back to his homeroom. He talked about not being the line leader. I empathized in my tone, body language, and words about how unfair that seemed and how disappointing he might feel. We discovered that the line leader was determined by alphabetical order. We wondered about when it would be his turn to be line leader and how patient and hopeful he could be.

Similar responses around disappointment continued to happen with Hydon for the next few weeks. Eventually, he could express his disappointment with words and decide to get a drink of water, go for a walk to feel better, talk to a friend (several friends volunteered to be his support person), ring the bell chimes, or draw it out. When he did throw something on the ground, he knew to pick it up and start again. He had greater tolerance and acceptance for the feeling of disappointment, a better understanding of his need for fairness behind the feeling of disappointment, and a wider vocabulary for expressing his challenges in waiting for his turn. This growth fed into his work projects, which he could now attend to with more focus and interest. I imagined how proud he might feel internally for handling such big emotions! He had a name for the emotion that most arose in him, he had confidence to say his need, and he had space to find solutions to his need. He had glimpsed an internal feedback loop of an emotion signaling a met or unmet need.

I believe I would have interfered in his spirit's will to focus on his area of learning that most needed attention (self-regulation) had I inserted my judgment, criticism, reprimand, and negative emotions. I also could have made his situation worse by insisting he get to (his academic) work. In fact, he was doing the work he most needed to do. It took him an extra three weeks to get to a place where he could complete his academic assignments peacefully next to a peer. In my mind, he had an A+ in growth and inspired me.

Given more time, I know we would have dug deeper into learning what words identified his emotions, where the emotions were being felt in his body (clenched jaw, upset stomach, etc.), which needs were behind the emotion, and how to care for his needs alongside others. He was growing in more harmony with himself and with others. He was self-perfecting. Thus, I believe that by nurturing this child's understanding of the connection between his emotional body, his mental body, and his physical body there was nurturance of his spirit.

Given more time in the schedule, I believe Hydon would have completed the remaining academic assignments too. Could my academic evaluations of him also be their own feedback loop, intrinsically driven and self-correcting? Could they help him look internally to self-perfection and exactitude? Could they assist him in learning more about himself? Could I give him an academic growth grade and a mastery grade? Yes, I could.

Within the Montessori approach, the general evaluation of work focuses on personal growth, rather than a set task due by a set target date. Some of the materials are self-correcting. Like a puzzle, the Montessori manipulatives used in math

72 Spirituality in the Classroom – What Do the Teachers Say?

guide the children to the correct answer and with more practice greater accuracy in their answers. The materials help the children form an internal visual of abstract concepts through repeated practice. They aid the children's inner development by their outer work. There is a faith, backed by Montessori's observation of children, that given nurturing guidance and a supportive environment to meet the full needs of the children, they will develop, by inner will, academically, emotionally, physically, and spiritually. With that nurturance, children will contribute to their well-being and the well-being of others and achieve mastery of skills. In *To Educate the Human Potential*, Maria Montessori shares,

> The child must learn by his own individual authority . . . and not to be questioned in his choice. Our teaching must only answer the mental needs of the child, not dictate them. He must have absolute freedom of choice and then he requires nothing but repeated experiences.
>
> *(2019, p. 7)*

As part of nurturing this self-perfection and self-awareness aspect of spirituality in the child, I have tried to meld the Montessori components of child-driven choice/work, varied practice, and ample time in my traditional public school setting of set curricular activities, set forms of practice, and set timetables. Engaging the children in research projects – stemming from their curiosity and wonder, rising from the presented curriculum, is one way I meld these practices. For example, in one of my classes, the children were learning about representation in U.S. Government. Several of the children wondered where all the indigenous people had gone. Many thought that they had all moved to a corner of Canada. They wanted to learn more. This off-shoot would take us off-schedule. Yet, the fiery curiosity in their eyes indicated to me this was their spirit's calling. "Can we do research about this, Ms. Escarfuller?" I opted to say yes. My class may temporarily 'fall behind' in the schedule or perhaps they may 'move ahead' in the curriculum because of their digging deeper into representation. I figured the tradeoff for falling behind schedule was nurturing their zest for learning and nurturing their inner will or spirit. I was giving them faith in their own development and internal calling.

Another example of helping the children tap into their spirituality through self-reflection, self-evaluation, and interaction with their environment comes from my first-grade class. The science curriculum we were following prompted the learning objective of describing how a plant part helps the whole plant survive and grow. I decided to add to our activities a song written by one of my Montessori trainers, Carla Foster, about the Parts of a Plant. We also choreographed a dance to go with the song. The children dissected plants of their choosing and labeled the plant parts. They wrote and illustrated their own Parts of the Plant books. We had various plants in the classroom and labeled their parts. We walked through the school garden and identified the parts of various garden plants. In each instance, the children were asked to choose what inspired and motivated them, pointing them inwardly to develop their self-awareness. In each instance, they self-evaluated their achievements, understanding, effort, and ability to communicate in their own words what they had learned.

Using movement, sound, and all their senses to embody their learning, they also learned more about themselves, their abilities, and their passions. Some were more into the dance, while others had a razor-sharp focus around meticulously dissecting and looking at the parts of the plant. As I shared earlier, this self-awareness is part of the process of self-perfection, of staying in line with your inner will and drive. Thus, it is also nurturing a child's spirituality.

In another area of the curriculum, studying positive and negative space, the children practiced repeatedly different combinations. As they looked at their work compared to the model, they answered the following questions: Did I create a line of symmetry? Did I balance each side of the page evenly? Was my work tidy? Did I give it my best effort? What would I choose to do differently? When they compared their first try to their final try, they saw growth in understanding symmetry, balance, and tidiness. Within the timeframe given in the curriculum, they did not all 'master' the skill, yet they all grew to a better understanding of the concept. They also had a better sense of their effort and of their desire to master the subject matter.

What about when a child shows their work: $2 + 2 = 7$? Surely, this is not perfect. The answer is not accurate, and yet perhaps the answer is perfect because it reveals that child's understanding. Perhaps the answer is also perfect because it reveals the child's cognitive processes to us. The answer is itself a 'feedback loop', a revelation of what is, an acceptance of that, and a guided redirection to truth. In the meantime, on a perfect day, the children have the time to reveal their understanding and then be guided to increased accuracy.

Sometimes, children ask me "Do you like it?" I aim to redirect the children to their own self-correcting wisdom. In her course, Katherine Winter-Sellery notes:

> that we are each governed internally means that we will enhance children's intrinsic motivation by withholding judgments about their achievements and instead inviting them to assess their own performances. We may add an opinion, but not a judgment (even when that judgment may be positive). This is because children experience even positive evaluations as being judgmental. This in turn can generate fear that they may not continue to measure up to our expectations.
>
> (Winter-Sellery et al., 2022b, p. 35)

So now I may respond "Congrats! You created it! How do you see your work?" or "You did it! What is your favorite part about your work?" In addition, I may walk

74 Spirituality in the Classroom – What Do the Teachers Say?

them through the assignment rubric/criteria and see how they grade themselves. I find that they usually have a clear sense of whether they are proud of their work or not; whether they did their best; and whether they understood the concepts taught. When not, I use the rubric to guide them on requirements of the assignment; they then have the option to make the necessary changes. Sometimes a child has decided not to change it, even if it meant a lower grade, because he/she liked it "a lot just like that!" The internal pride in their work overrode the external grade. And by keeping my own judgment out of the equation they stayed that much more internally driven, self-directed, and self-perfecting. In that way, I fed their spirituality by guiding them to listen to the voice within each of them.

Purpose

"Our observation of children has made us realize that work is man's fundamental instinct and that a child can work from morning till night without ever feeling tired, as if his labor were part of the order of nature" (Montessori, 2015, p. 92). Maria Montessori observed that when children were given certain carefully prepared materials, they were naturally compelled toward them, as if by some inner drive and self-will. I remember a PreK lesson around the shapes in the natural world, in which I introduced the children to the Montessori Primary (three-to six-year-old) Geometric Cabinet, full of shapes for the children to trace and touch with their hands. This cabinet is full of a variety of circles, triangles, and quadrilaterals. The children wide-eyed patiently waited their turn to practice with a shape. After they each had a turn with at least one, it was time for me to end the 45-minute lesson. The next day, I returned and presented another lesson and activity around shapes for them to do. Many children opted to return to the Geometric Cabinet instead. They each were completely engaged and worked tirelessly in their chosen activity.

I regret the many times I interrupt a child's concentration so that he/she would do 'my assignment' and the missed opportunity for nurturing his/her personal embodied learning. It is quite the juggling act to meet the needs of the child's inner drive and spirit, meet the academic standards set, and keep up with the pacing of a public school education.

It's All in Our Favor

For me, 'it's all in our favor' goes back to the idea that everything is perfect just the way it is. It takes deep faith in the child, and in humanity, to believe that everything he/she is undergoing is part of Spirit's plan. It is far easier for me to embrace this idea for the child yelling, throwing a chair, hitting a friend with a pencil, or just balling up his work and throwing it in the trash bin. It is harder when feeling the weight of my regrets as an educator to think 'It's all in our favor'. I regret so many of my actions in the classroom; when I have assumed the worst, when I shamed, judged, or criticized a child to motivate them. Yes, in those moments, I have a difficult time reconciling that it's all in our favor (perfectly suited to our realignment with Spirit) when I think I have been a hindrance to a child's development, when I've added more gunk to his/her inner world.

Thankfully, through the course with Katherine Winter-Sellery of Conscious Parenting Revolution (Winter-Sellery et al., 2022a), I have learned to understand these reactions to those moments as 'tragic expressions' of unmet needs. I understood the 'not yet peaceful' child – aka the children traditionally labeled 'bad' or 'difficult' because of their disruptive behavior (Goertz, 2000), and it was Katherine's training that gave me the lightbulb moment. I now had the step-by-step language, brought forth from Katherine Winter-Sellery's training in Non-Violent Communication (NVC) by Marshall Rosenberg to help the children unwind their tightly tied knots of emotion, and to express their needs in a more productive way that would build instead of destroy connection, a language free of judgment and full of validation. The step-by-step process involved creating a judgment-free mindset in me first, then within each moment of 'tragic expression':

1. setting my personal needs aside to attend to the child;
2. guiding the child to identify what she/he experienced sensorially;
3. what she/he thought at that moment;
4. what emotions arose from within the child; and
5. what needs were behind those emotions.

When I used this NVC language consistently, I noticed the classroom being more self-managed and an increase in children's ability to problem solve, see the other and empathize, and above all feel relief in being seen, heard, understood, and met just as they were. A calm confidence began to settle in the children. They had an increased ability to concentrate on work and to handle any emotion that arose. I will share more in Chapter 5 about how one child's growth has impacted me and everyone in his class.

This concrete language gave me the words to express how we as spirit are perfect, and of full worth even though our thoughts, emotions, and sensations may have us thinking otherwise. Instead of "I am angry!", the children were heard saying "I got angry in me!" or "Anger is rising up in me!" or asking each other "What's that anger about?" We talked about how wise our body is in finding where this emotion is – a clenched jaw, a hot face, a tight fist – and how we could 'catch it'. We made it okay. We came up with different ways to listen to our emotions safely. Now, we could figure out what the unmet need was behind the emotion. They began to see their emotions as neither good nor bad, rather as helpers to get our needs met. They saw that they could help each other out, empathize, and be bigger than their emotions.

76 Spirituality in the Classroom – What Do the Teachers Say?

We Are Spiritual Beings, Energy, and Manifesters

I extended this separation of our identity from our emotions to other aspects of humanity. My pedagogical language began to change and to reflect my understanding of spirit communicating through embodied nature of man through nine distinct aspects. Now I aim to replace 'I am' with:

1. My body feels . . . (physical)
2. This emotion arising in me . . . (emotional)
3. I (saw, heard, smelled, tasted, touched/felt) (sensorial)
4. My mind began to think . . . (mental)
5. I remembered . . . (memories)
6. I believe 'I rock' . . . (belief)
7. My capacity . . . (natural abilities)
8. I require . . . and others require (needs)
9. My choice to meet my needs is . . . (will)

For example, by shifting the language from 'I am angry' to 'I feel anger in me', I intend to gently guide them to remember that they are Spirit, not their emotions, thoughts, or sensations, hopefully breeding opportunities for them to see themselves as whole and complete just as they are. I hope that they see these aspects of humanity as tools which they may become skilled at using to align with their individual spirits or souls. I know shifting my lens and voicing in this language has helped, and continues to help, me release judgment more quickly and I see myself slowly and steadily blossoming into a gentler and more compassionate educator and person.

> When we know we are energy beings, we begin to live away from the fear-based stories our minds create and start living from the other option that is available to us – the perspective of our true, eternal nature as the Soulful Self.
> *(Morter, 2019, p. 19)*

Believing that the goal of education is to create greater justice, peace, and harmonious joy in our world, I became more conscious of my language in the classroom. My Montessori training already mentioned the critical aspect of the teacher's words, actions, and tones. When I understood that on the quantum level our words do produce and are a form of psychic energy (thoroughly described in *The Biology of Belief* by Bruce Lipton), I became even more conscious of my language in the classroom environment. What kind of energy did I want to create in the classroom, in myself. Synthesizing my previous learning with learning in Katherine Winter-Sellery's course in the Conscious Parenting Revolution, I learned that an aspect of a nurturing spiritual language becomes the language of fundamental human needs; it is the language of 'I wonder', 'I feel', 'I need',

How Ms. Escarfuller's Spirituality Informs Her Pedagogy **77**

and 'I have' this emotion arising in me. This is spiritual language because it communicates the universal truth of who we are. We turn our attention from 'right or wrong' to 'what is the basic human need demanding to be met'.

> It absolutely doesn't work to try to stuff our feelings and impose calm. What we resist persists! . . . Instead, we learn three little words. Something in me. Something in you. When we develop this language internally as our inner dialogue or outside ourselves when others are upset, we shift our whole perspective from large to small. We get bigger than what's bugging us. Just three little words! . . . Being bigger leads to compassion and compassion leads to natural change, not forcing or denying it. It's not the words that make the change. The change happens because you use the words to help shift your attention.
>
> *(Winter-Sellery et al., 2022b, p. 62)*

I have revisited Katherine Winter-Sellery's workbook many times, as she expands on the internal language of our thoughts, how to create pathways that help identify our needs and how to meet our needs in a way that builds connection with others. I still have many 'oops!' moments, as Faith Bost (2020) calls 'tragic expressions' in her Conscious Language course, and I am incrementally expanding my capacity for receiving all emotions compassionately.[1] I refer you to her course and workbook to have an accurate and detailed picture of the process of creating this energy in your environment, an environment full of safety that all needs will be met. Here, true learning can thrive. Where we are thriving and growing, I believe we are connecting with our Highest Self, and thus nurturing our spirituality. Through a shift in language, we were creating a new reality in the classroom. I also wanted the children to have a visual in their minds of their powerful Spirit. I wanted them to connect that their words, subsequent thoughts, and emotions were energy. They were manifesting through their words because they too were energy or Spirit. Dr. Peggy Jenkins, in *Nurturing Spirituality in Children in the Non-Sectarian Classroom*, gives us several activities to concretize for the children this abstract concept of being Spirit. In one of the activities, there is a bowl of water filled with ice and we say to the children

> the ice cubes represent all people, and the water represents Spirit, the invisible power of the Universe. Water can take form – the form of ice. Spirit, which is invisible can also take form and become visible. We are visible forms of Spirit.
>
> *(1995, p. 19)*

I was building that connection that as Spirit, our words, thoughts, and emotions can become visible too.

Holding these beliefs and living from them is akin to knowing exercise is healthy for you and actually exercising. Sometimes I do and sometimes I don't.

78 Spirituality in the Classroom – What Do the Teachers Say?

Each day is a new beginning to form a habit. Seeing these young children, ages three to 12, learn these concepts, put them into practice, and then see their increased peacefulness and confidence gives me much reason to hope.

Full, Complete, and Equal

In 1997, I first started teaching in Minneapolis as an Art Educator, for grades K–8. I had just completed a traditional teaching program. Maria Montessori was a passing historical figure in the history of education class. I remember the children as being 'clean vessels' for us to pour information into. I learned that they needed to be managed, disciplined, and 'made to listen'. Like in most classrooms, I had rewards and punishments. I managed my classroom well and the children behaved. Except there was one problem – I did not enjoy disciplining and management as I had learned to do it. I was constantly dishing out judgment disguised as rewards and punishments when I did not like to be judged. I was forcing obedience through threats of calling home, loss of recess, and receiving a scowl from me. This form of classroom discipline drained me, and I decided to leave education. I did not want to be this way with others; I was doing unto others what I did not want done to me. I knew who I wanted to be character wise and that was not it! I had much unlearning to do.

When my firstborn was about to enter kindergarten, I had to lean into education again. Did I want my son to enter the same system I had left? Did I want my son to be potentially disciplined by school police, or to have little to no choice to self-direct his learning and personal needs (bathroom, meals)? I decided to homeschool him. Not that I knew much better then or had gained the necessary skills to act from my Highest Self. I figured my home was safer than the other options I knew existed. In this decision, I searched the Internet and discovered a plethora of 'alternative progressive education' models. A friend from my son's preschool encouraged me to visit a Montessori classroom. From the start, I was hooked. The natural calm, joyful, and engaged activity in these three- to six-year-olds astounded me. I attempted to model my homeschool curriculum around the Montessori aspects I understood at that time: ample time for the child to engage in work uninterrupted, and natural materials for the child to manipulate (e.g., glass, wood, fabric, clay). The following year he enrolled in a Montessori school. When he was of age, my other child also enrolled. I enjoyed having the blessing to send my two children to Montessori schools for some time. I was becoming – in minuscule ways – a gentler kinder parent and person. My interest in teaching in the public school system was also being rekindled. I had glimpsed a path guiding me to embody my Highest Self and to be a loving presence for children to be as well. Even if it would take me a lifetime to get to my Highest Self, I was excited to have a roadmap to get there. May the journey begin!

In 2016, I entered Montessori training and discovered (no surprise here) I had much to unlearn. My evolution continues still and is one reason why I now enjoy my journey as a teacher; I learn so much from the children and I see how they learn from me. I share the phrase of one of my trainers, Carla Foster, with the children: "Everybody helps everybody." I remind them that 'everybody' includes me. They know they can help me grow too. When I have an 'oops' or 'ouch' moment, and I accept the children redirecting me, they feel empowered and visible. In turn they are more receptive to feedback; a trust has been built that we can rely on each other. They know they have something to contribute that we all grapple with challenging emotions and thoughts that give rise to these emotions. We all have some triggers, our debilitating thoughts, and desire to meet our needs. We can model for each other how to respond to build connection and recenter ourselves, to align with Spirit.

Initially, I thought my classroom would be a chaotic anarchy if I gave the children choice and voice. Would they really be naturally cooperative? Would they really be self-directed and desire to work? Giving way to trust in Montessori theory allowed me to witness a classroom that began to be self-directed and self-managing. When the children were taught the different jobs for managing the classroom, they were eager to take them on. The children were empowered to bring the class to attention at the beginning and end of the day. They led class meeting. They tidied the classroom. They cleaned up after themselves. They soothed each other at a peace table. They moved from one work into another work independently. They also worked together and assisted each other. I would teach a lesson to some children, and then I would observe them teach it to a friend. For example, I would teach them how to play the Stamp Game (used primarily for static and dynamic addition and subtraction) and they would then invite another child to play (aka work) with them. The children would read to each other and edit each other's work. If a child needed help sweeping the floor or dusting the materials on a shelf, there were peers willing to assist.

In other ways, I do still find it challenging to give the children their full natural autonomy within the schedule and protocols of the school day. For example, I would love to guide them to manage their own snacks, bathroom breaks, and materials, yet the requirement to keep everyone safe in a large setting, share resources, and manage time efficiently sometimes manifests as eating only at a certain time, going to the bathroom at a set time, and keeping all the materials on teacher's shelf. For now, I assert myself empathetically saying, "I understand you. However, I (or the school) need(s). . . . So, what can we do about that?" (Winter-Sellery et al., 2022b, p. 186). We end up finding a solution.

Needs, Mattering, and Growth

While meeting the children's physical needs in the classroom like safety, nutrition, expression, and work seemed more concrete and straightforward, meeting the spiritual needs such as belonging, connection, mattering, and autonomy was

80 Spirituality in the Classroom – What Do the Teachers Say?

vaguer to me in a system that dictates most decisions for the child. As previously mentioned, my Montessori training shifted how I saw my role as an educator. I became a guide assisting the child to meet his/her needs, both physical and spiritual. The child was no longer an 'empty vessel' which I needed to teach he/she to become a complete and adequate being. Instead, I was guiding a spirit, a soul, to awaken to his/her wholeness and worth in human form. With each passing day, I grow, evolve, and discover what that means for me, for my actions with the children, and for the school community.

More and more, I pause to listen to see what questions show up and to observe before I interject. I empower more instead of controlling and leading every activity. For example, instead of inspecting the clean-up of the classroom, I invite a few of the children to supervise the clean-up. Instead of scolding the children for their expressions of anger, I invite them to tell me about it. Instead of moving forward with the curriculum, I attend to the curiosities that arise apart from the curriculum. I may not yet understand the nuances of why this all works to create more harmonious, productive, and engaged children in the classroom yet when I see their cooperation, enthusiasm, curiosity, and desire to resolve conflicts peacefully, I imagine that their spirituality has been nurtured.

In Montessori, we share with the children that fundamental needs, such as artistic expression, food, community, and movement, are constant through all stages of human development. We share that these fundamental needs apply to everyone, across race, country borders, and culture. We share with the children that the Universe has work to do and rules to follow to satisfy these needs; Maria Montessori called it 'the cosmic task'. This 'cosmic task' means, in the Montessori context, that each thing in the Universe is here to fulfill its purpose. As each thing in the Universe satisfies its needs to serve its purpose, it also contributes to the greater good. For example, when a plant satisfies its need for food, by making its own food through photosynthesis, it gives off oxygen into the air. This 'oxygen' waste contributes to our existence since this is what we require to live. In turn, we release the carbon dioxide the plant requires. Everyone, here the plant and human being, engaged in their 'cosmic task' benefits the whole. We may not be conscious of how we are contributing and still, we are. This interdependence and connectedness points to a greater Source of all creation. It points to Spirit. The more conscious we are aware of this interdependence and connectedness, the more careful we will be to act responsibly toward ourselves, others, and our environment. For me, this inspires cooperation and consideration, and reverence for the other. It motivates me to nurture my spirituality and children's spirituality in the classroom.

One way we make this concept in the Montessori classroom more tangible is through storytelling. Starting in first grade, we say that the human being came with three basic gifts: the 'mind to think', the 'heart to love', and the 'hand to work'. Then, we say that those gifts are guided toward our purpose with our 'tendencies',

How Ms. Escarfuller's Spirituality Informs Her Pedagogy **81**

which for me are a manifestation of spirit. She believed that as embodied human beings we have not only simple physical needs but also spiritual needs. These spiritual needs drive us to evolve, grow, and connect to something outside ourselves. They drive us to create and manifest something new in our world, our religions, art, music, celebrations, inventions, and all our constructions. Everything we have created has been driven by our desire to meet both physical and spiritual needs. Maria Montessori called our human creations the 'sopranatura' or 'supernature'.

> Why are beehives called the work of nature while the paved roads built by man are not? Why does a cow belong to nature, but a chemical retort does not? . . . Because man goes further. He creates artificial things in nature. He extracts water from rocks and carries it to living creatures. He mines the earth for iron, coal, gold, and precious stones and brings them to the surface. Man is the creator of a supernature. He is the master of matter. He has learned to exploit sources of energy lying deep below the surface of the earth and is using them for the creation of the supernature. But he is aware of only individual phenomena and his mind does not grasp their essence. . . . He is more intelligent, but the feelings that should accompany this increase in intelligence are still missing. . . . Nobler feelings – awareness of the unity of all living beings, for instance – are very slowly appearing in him. But harmony has yet to be achieved. . . . As supernature is being constructed the evolution of man is also taking place, representing not only the further evolution of nature, but also a development of human personality. . . . The child must therefore find a teacher able to develop his higher instincts.
>
> *(Montessori, 2015, pp. 92–93)*

No matter where we live this is the case; we have the needs of the physical body, and we have the needs of the spiritual 'body.' Our spirit compels us to meet all of our needs even if we are not conscious of it, growing and evolving along the way as we aim to live from a thriving state of joy, love, and unity. In the process, we create something new.

Montessori Human Tendencies and Pedagogy

In 1956, Mario M. Montessori held a lecture in the Netherlands about the human tendencies, which has been reprinted as a pamphlet by AMI: *The Human Tendencies and Montessori Education* in which he writes

> To her, the word (adaptation) meant happiness, ease, and the sort of inner equilibrium which gives a sense of security to the child. It is based on the permanency of the spiritual, ethical, and economical equilibrium of the group environment in which his family both lives and has a very determined social standing. . . .

82 Spirituality in the Classroom – What Do the Teachers Say?

From this point of view the conditions of our present make it much more difficult for the child to become adapted than formerly. Now-a-days not only in one nation but in the whole world society seems to be in a state of chaos, due both to the impact of new and conflicting ideas which come from all sides – and to economical, social, and spiritual changes that have occurred in the near past. So, the general feeling is that no longer is anything permanent. All feel insecure: not only individuals but also nations. It is not extraordinary therefore that in such conditions children find it more difficult to become adapted than previously.

(Montessori, 1956, p. 1)

In reading *The Human Tendencies and Montessori Education*, I came to understand that Maria Montessori taught that to meet our needs human beings are given tendencies, such as movement and work/activity; these tendencies are a type of inner compass guiding us to meet our needs and to evolve. For me, I see these tendencies, or behaviors, as expressions of spirit, quietly awakening us to our individual will and best, adapting us to our Highest Self, or spiritual self. Through this book and my Montessori training, I have understood thus far that the tendencies have the following in common:

1. they are fundamental and constant;
2. they are always present (not created or destroyed);
3. they are common to all of us, crossing all borders;
4. they shape our human behavior;
5. they help each of us adapt, evolve, and to create a new way of life within our lifetime;
6. they compel us to act and thus ensure we meet our needs;
7. they are always active (never dormant); and
8. they manifest themselves differently at different developmental stages of life.[2]

My learning about human tendencies and growing to be able to recognize them in the children's actions and expressions continues to be essential in shaping my pedagogy and my classroom environment. To learn more about Montessori's views about human tendencies, please refer to Mario Montessori's *The Human Tendencies and Montessori Education*, as well as her other books referenced at the end of this chapter; I give you a synopsis of my current understanding of these tendencies here:

Movement: We want to move from birth. Movement is how we engage our other tendencies and build connections within ourselves and with others.

Exploration: Exploration is the desire to investigate our inner world and external world. Having our physical needs met, we move more toward exploring our inner world (of emotions, thoughts, beliefs, etc.).

Curiosity: This is our desire to know and understand our world. Here lie our questions; Why? How? Who? This curiosity keeps us mentally and physically active and helps us find meaning.

Orientation: This is the ability to find one's way and to situate oneself, may it be physically, emotionally, intellectually, or socially. It gives us a sense of security and connection.

Order: Order helps us feel secure that we will have our needs met. We can rely on resources being available to us when we require them. Having external order helps us to order internally.

Observation: Observation helps us understand our world accurately. Montessori believed it was what aided us to develop the scientific mind, the mind based on objectivity and facts.

Imitation: Human beings like to copy. We learn and understand by mimicking. According to Montessori, they imitate "to adapt to this world and be able to do all things done in the environment" (Montessori, 2012, p. 119).

Abstraction: Abstraction connects to order. It is having an internal visual of concepts.

> The children have '. . . for themselves something which we could not transmit by words alone. We give them an abstraction . . . to understand this abstract concept by using the material. We call this mechanism materialized abstraction.
> *(Montessori, 2012, p. 70)*

Concretely, at the age of three the child uses the division board to 'share out' beads evenly among the pegs. Abstraction is achieved when they have internalized the concept and can now do division with pencil and paper without the use of the concrete materials. In the Elementary grades, ages six to 12, this involves holding the morals, virtues, and ideas of the group in your mind and acting accordingly.

Concentration: Concentration permits us to hold our attention on something despite distractions. It is connected to observation and helps us to abstract and learn. For example, the Cylinders material, enticing to as early as the one-and-a-half-year-old, gives a concrete presentation of dimensionality. Maria Montessori states:

> If you were to give a child the set that varies in three dimensions, you will find that he can put a cylinder into the wrong cavity and subsequently will be unable to get it out again. . . . Such activity would cause the constructive interest to be lost. It is therefore best to give him the set where the difference is in two dimensions. As all the cylinders in the set have the same height, the little knob is easy is always easy to hold even if the cylinders were misplaced. This will enable the child to correct himself. . . . the attention is held through the

84 Spirituality in the Classroom – What Do the Teachers Say?

eye, which takes in the difference . . . with these exact instruments the child's mind is forced to remain attentive.

(Montessori, 2012, pp. 71–72)

Imagination: The mind is driven to imagine what is not there, to see what is not available to the senses. Everything man-made first started in someone's imagination. It helps us create in our external and internal world. For example, imagining ourselves back in times of happy memories puts us in an internal, emotional state of happiness.

Work/Activity: For any idea to be translated into reality, work is required. The heart and mind depend on the hand (body) to manifest their musings. Work, even play as work, has intentionality and purpose in nurturing spirituality in the child as well as his/her physical, emotional, and mental faculties. This is connected to movement. Maria Montessori noted:

We must let the child walk and notice how he walks. . . . The attention of little children is continually being drawn to one thing or another in their walks. . . . They stop to observe and admire things they see. . . . This is a preparation for the adaptation to the environment. The absorption of the environment is an intellectual activity. It is a psychic necessity that the child explores the environment; it satisfies his spirit . . . in this way a child could walk for miles.

(Montessori, 2012, p. 130)

Exactness: Exactness moves us to try again and again. We use this when we aim for precision in our communication, our plans, our movements, or 'to get it right'. One way we see this is in our aim to communicate with more clarity our ideas, feelings, and needs.

Repetition: Repetition is how we refine and internalize our learning. From age zero to six, exploring the same concept with the same material over and over may be very appealing. For the elementary child, from ages six to 12, repetition manifests as the practice of the same concept with a variety of materials. For example, these children may practice addition with the Addition Strip board, the Stamp Game, or the Bank Game to name a few.

Self-perfection: We want to give our best; our spirit always does. When a child continues to practice his soccer ball dribbles to create a unique style to his moves, that is self-perfection. When they practice their handwriting until they have their name just as they would like it, that is self-perfection. This is connected to exactness and repetition.

Calculation: Calculation helps us predict, measure, and quantify. It helps us sequence, order, and abstract. When a child sees how many earths fit in the Earth, or how many triangles make a square he/she is using calculation.

Gregariousness: We are social beings. We learn and grow together. Creating opportunities for six- to 12-year-old to have debates, discussions, interviews, and surveys supports this tendency and builds upon the natural desire for connection.

Communication: Communication is tied to gregariousness; we need to communicate. Communication happens on many levels, both verbal and non-verbal, physical, and spiritual. Communication is necessary to work, play, and live together harmoniously.

Self-control: This is the ability to manage the body, mind, and heart to act in harmony with the environment, whether physical, social, or spiritual. With self-control, impulses and urges can be managed and delayed. It is related to self-awareness and character development. The adolescent knows they can drive at 90 mph but chooses to honor the speed limit. The three-year-old wants a drink of water and can wait for her/his turn to use the water fountain.

Knowing that these tendencies have been studied and documented by many from many perspectives and over many years, my aim was to share my own humble understanding of all of these and how they inform my pedagogy; I refer you to Maria Montessori's *The 1946 London Lectures* (2012), and her other books, to investigate more on how she saw each of these. Since these tendencies are always operating in us and our children, they must also guide my work with them. Keeping these needs and tendencies in mind, we can better observe the spirit of the child, the inner life of the child that holds his/her gift to the Universe. We can better nurture the child's spirit and know we are nurturing his gifts to create greater harmony instead of harm, to peace instead of war. Education must acknowledge and support the tendencies at each stage of development if we are to nurture the spirituality of children. We as educators, according to my Montessori training, can do several things to nurture these tendencies, urges of spirit:

1. we can remove obstacles in the environment that hinder these tendencies;
2. we can adapt the environment to support the tendencies as they manifest at each developmental stage of the child;
3. we prepare the environment with care, rehearsing within the environment as if we were the child; and
4. we prepare ourselves methodically to give our best.

As described earlier with the dimensions work of the Cylinders material, we give appropriate challenges so the child may operate with motivation. If the challenge is too little or too much frustration, boredom or resignation may be one of the outcomes, respectively. The classroom goes silent, and the children seem to lack motivation. Being aware of the tendencies helps me understand why putting our focus on the spirituality of children, not the curriculum, is the most important. This allows them to feel safe enough to learn, to feel the desire to explore, and to give the best of themselves. As Dr. Mata shared in one of our many book-writing conversations,

> While the spirit is embodied it speaks through human needs. Human needs are how spirit speaks through us. Spirit is manifesting through these needs. We create with our highest self when we meet needs with love, curiosity, empathy, harmony The difference from my Best Self and my Highest Self. I will still hinder them [children/students] from my best self, and that is still ok, it's part of the journey; the child is in my classroom because it's meant to be. The goal is to nurture from my highest self, instead of just with my best self in order to best meet the needs of the child.

In sum, nurturing children's spirituality in, and through, education matters because I desire to contribute to greater connection with others, self, and nature and to have more justice and harmony, and compassionate action. I strive to act from this place so I may contribute toward creating that reality.

Notes

1. Remember, I had previously been trying to fix my emotions of fear, anger, and sadness that I had come to believe should not be expressed. In addition, I believed at a young age that expressing my needs was a burden.
2. For example, a three-year-old tendency for work manifests in the repeated continuous polishing of a shoe well after it has been polished, and simply because of the movement involved in polishing while an eight-year-old tendency for work manifests as getting the shoe polished to her/his satisfaction.

References

Bost, F. (2020). *Conscious language workbook.* Retrieved November 1, 2022, from https://faithinwellness.com

Cavalletti, S. (1978). *The spiritual development of the child, Montessori talks to parents* (p. 14). North American Montessori Teacher's Association.

Goertz, D. (2000). *Children who are not yet peaceful: Preventing exclusion in the early elementary classroom.* Frog Books.

Jenkins, P. J. (1995). *Nurturing spirituality in children* (p. 6). Beyond Words Publishing.

Lipton, B. (2016). *Biology of belief, unleashing the power of consciousness, matter, and miracles.* Hay House.

Montessori, M. (2001). *The advanced Montessori method* (Vol. 1). Clio Press.

Montessori, M. (2007). *The discovery of the child* (Vol. 2). Montessori-Pierson.

Montessori, M. (2012). *The 1946 London lectures* (p. 70, 71–72, 119, 130). Montessori-Pierson.

Montessori, M. (2015). *Education and peace* (The Montessori Series, Vol. 10, pp. 34, 92–93). Montessori-Pierson.

Montessori, M. (2019). *To educate the human potential* (The Montessori Series, Vol. 6, p. 7). Montessori-Pierson.

Montessori, M. M. (1956). *The human tendencies and Montessori Education* (p. 1). Associación Montessori Internationale.

Montessori, M. M. (2008). *Education for human development: Understanding Montessori.* Montessori-Pierson.

Morter, S. (2019). *The energy codes, the 7 step system to awaken your spirit, heal your body, and live your best life* (p. 19). ATRIA Books.

Rosenblum, B., & Kuttner, F. (2011). *Quantum enigma: Physics encounters consciousness.* Oxford University Press.

Winter-Sellery, K., Porter, L., & Jamieson, C. N. (2022a). *Conscious parenting revolution course.* Retrieved November 1, 2022, from https://consciousparentingrevolution.com/.

Winter-Sellery, K., Porter, L., & Jamieson, C. N. (2022b). *Conscious parenting revolution workbook* (pp. 35, 62, 186). Retrieved May 2, 2022, from https://consciousparenting-revolution.com/

Wolf, A. D. (1996). *Nurturing the spirit in the non-sectarian classrooms* (p. 10). Parent Child Press. www.montessoriservices.com

5

VIGNETTES FROM MS. ESCARFULLER'S CLASSROOM

As I offer vignettes of nurturing spirituality in my various classrooms and educator roles, I hope they inspire and encourage you to reach out and share your best practices too. Through these vignettes of my work with children, ages three to 10 (PreK-third grade), in an inner-city Title 1[1] public school setting may a dialogue further open toward greater efficacy in nurturing a child's spirituality as our own. With this dialogue, may a conversation in nurturing spirituality in secular settings move incrementally closer to being a daily topic in educator talk, as is curriculum, and grades.

Choice: The Material Serves the Child

In my traditional public school setting, I observed Leno, a three-year-old wide-eyed boy with a quiet smile. He attentively watched my lessons and after each lesson, he would return to the Geometric Cabinet, filled with various wooden shapes (see Figure 5.1). He kept tracing just one shape, first the largest circle, then the triangle, and so forth. Every day for three weeks he went to the same activity (see Figure 5.2). From time to time, I nudged him to complete the activity from my lesson so I could enter the required weekly grades; standards required completion by a certain time. He obliged and then returned to his inner will's calling. This spontaneous call compelled him to move in the direction of the Geometric Cabinet; concentrated movement signaling spirituality in action. Instead of the child serving the academic materials, the academic materials were serving the child; instead of the child being forced to work with the material, the materials worked for the child.

DOI: 10.4324/9781003081463-8

FIGURE 5.1 Child Geometric Cabinet work

Source: Patricia Escarfuller

FIGURE 5.2 Child repeating work

Source: Patricia Escarfuller

The spontaneous purposeful movement toward an object with deliberate steps in quiet contentment appeared, drawn out by the lessons previously presented to him. I afforded him independent access to all the materials required for him to repeat this work as often as he willed. With repetition, his right hand increased its abilities in exactness and perfection of his fine motor movement.

Another opportunity to witness the will of the child being served by the material occurred on an outdoor painting day. After deciding individually that they were done with their painting work, the children would each clean up after themselves. Then, they had a choice of outdoor work in which to engage. Some watered plants, some went down the slides, and some engaged with each other. One girl continuously washed her palette and painting rag (see Figure 5.3).

FIGURE 5.3 Child engaged in washing

Source: Patricia Escarfuller

She would dip and ring her rag, scrub her palette, and start again. Other children would gather, and she continued her work as if no one was watching. When it was time to go, I gently reminded her that she needed to clean up her work. She had been washing for about 20 minutes. I would have loved to see her get to a satisfactory completion of her task instead of her task being declared completed because of time.

Hands at Work

In one of my third-grade art classes, most of the children asked for the opportunity to sew their own pillow by hand,[2] a project that could cross various curricular areas. Several of the boys who had challenges staying on an assigned task refused to participate. One opted for drumming, one opted for sketching, and one did not want to work with any material available. This child, Nester, walked around the room and chatted with peers engaged in their sewing. One day, he shared that he knew he could not make a pillow. "Thank goodness your hands do not have ears! They probably want to give it a go," I joked. Encouraged by his peers, he started. He stopped and started. Yes, we acknowledged that holding the small needle had its challenges. Yes, it hurt when the needle pierced your skin. Then one day, something clicked, and he went to a quiet corner and sewed nonstop for 30 minutes until the period was over; he wanted more time. Fortunately, it was my planning time so I could stay with him and the next teacher, happy to see him engaged in work, permitted him to continue. He went back to his corner while I worked on the other end of the room at a table grading student work. He came up to me wide-eyed and a giant smile on his face (see Figure 5.4). "I didn't think I could do it and then I thought what if I thought I can, so I persisted, and I did it!" He made two more pillows, for family members, and helped other children finish theirs. Later on, he was hired to sew back together a sweatshirt pocket section for a middle school child for five dollars. He had found a gift hidden in his hands.

Movement Revealing

Our second-grade classroom was organized to have various seating arrangements, for individual work and various-sized group work. There were rugs and low tables for working on the floor, round tables for group work, and individual desks near windows. Materials were placed by category and curricular area rather than by assignment; for example, all the paper, whether for art, writing, or math, were in one area. The children had the responsibility to move with purpose to gather and acquire whatever material they needed to complete their work and then to clean up their work, returning all the materials to their original locations. We had a central rug, around which we gathered campfire style, sharing stories

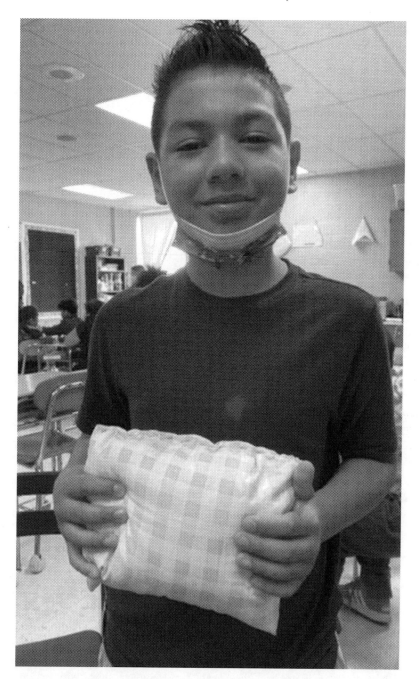

FIGURE 5.4 Child hand sews his first pillow
Source: Patricia Escarfuller

about real-life heroes, singing tunes, and celebrating each other. It's also where we problem-solved community challenges surrounding fairness, and other issues that arose. We had a peace area (see Figure 5.5) for problem-solving conflicts safely, and a quiet zone for attunement to one's emotions and thoughts. The goal of these arrangements was for the child to have the ability to move with a purpose for work and choice as to where to complete that work. Also, this varied seating and spaces would reveal to whom and to what material the child was attracted and reveal aspects of his/her personality.

FIGURE 5.5 Peace area

Source: Jennifer Mata-McMahon

Gregariousness & Conversation

In the beginning of the school year, my high expectations need to be communicated. In addition, some harmonious order and community need to be created among my assigned group of elementary children, strangers to each other and me. How do I establish these two things?

At the start, we have a small group brainstorm around how we wanted to feel in school and what we needed to feel that way; we worked starting from emotion first and then identified the need behind it, such as safety, or belonging. One child, Nathan, a first grader, began to come into my focus amid the lively buzz of discussion. His voice was low as he moved from his table and approached each

94 Spirituality in the Classroom – What Do the Teachers Say?

of the other groups. I saw his hands moving to open palm posture and lean in to ask a question of a peer. I observed him looking at writing on note catcher chart paper for each group. He ping-ponged like this for a short while between tables. In the meantime, I wondered why he was not at his table. Did his group not have any ideas? Did he not like the people with whom he had been randomly grouped? How was his group going to get their work done without his input? How was he contributing? A fear arose in me around being judged on my 'classroom management.' Why had I not made the child sit down? Why was he still walking around? I mustered every seed of restraint available to ride the fear-based urge to interrupt him and stayed in observation mode.

The other children continued their work, sometimes smiling and nodding to him as he approached or spoke; the flow of work continued. I felt relief when we gathered back to share our findings and we were, in my mind, all "properly seated." One person would stand up and patiently make the peace sign to signal for silence, then speak for his/her group once he/she had the floor. Each group shared around their needs for safety, learning, fun, kindness, and support.

I realized that each group chose to focus on rules in specific locations of our campus such as the classroom, the cafeteria, the library, and the playground. I had not given that instruction. Nathan had orchestrated covering every possible area in the school. Did the rule seem fair in that location? Then if not, we had to change it. "Well, we can't say quiet feet in school because we need to run around at recess. But we want to be safe so that we don't get bumped or hurt or break something and then have a cut and . . . so we just need to watch our feet wherever we go so we don't bother anyone," he explained. Nathan revealed his capacity for problem-solving frustration, for openness to other perspectives, and for compromise.

After that, he called on each group and they discussed and voted whether to include the rule in our contract. I guided in rephrasing what you don't want as what you need; "no bossing people around" became "ask for what you need with kindness." We drafted our rules into a contract identifying our needs to feel safe, loved, and appreciated and worded them to support our inner qualities, such as helpfulness and kindness, and then we each signed it with our favorite pen (see Figure 5.6); Nathan signed it last.

While he appeared shy to speak in front of the group before, in this scenario he oozed ease and a confident presence. At that moment, he became the leader to whom everyone gravitated when challenging social conflicts arose. He became our advisor and our peacemaker. I was in humble awe of his ability to understand and empathize with his peers at seven years of age. Here again, spirituality was revealed to me, perhaps one of his spirit's purposes in life. Of his own volition and given the time and space to exercise his will, he showed who he was. Giving room to movement and gregariousness, we all received the gift of Nathan's diplomacy.

FIGURE 5.6 Classroom Contract
Source: Jennifer Mata-McMahon

Time & Pacing

Strict pacing and blocked time stand as current logistical realities in my traditional public school setting. This pacing issue was present in one of my third-grade Social Studies classes. This section of the curriculum had us covering Early America (colonists) with no background about women, children, indigenous people, or enslaved people. Some students asked, "Where did all the indigenous people go?" I gave it to the group to answer. They offered, "Well, they were all killed off." "They all died from diseases or from being shot." "They were shoved off their land into a corner of Canada where they still live." Then one child asked, "Can we do research again and make our own books?" Would I satisfy this eagerness, curiosity, imagination, and empathy for the seemingly invisible other or stay on track with the set curriculum tasks? Staying on track seemed like telling the children to eat broccoli at their birthday party and eat their birthday cake another day; their cake was the indigenous people, their broccoli, and the handouts from the curriculum.

I incorporated some additional information the next day on indigenous people. A colleague gave me some authentic books to support the children's desire to research the indigenous people of this country. They demonstrated interest to

96 Spirituality in the Classroom – What Do the Teachers Say?

jump into their research, yet they had a Representation Project the curriculum required them to complete by a set date. What inspiration of creativity would help me merge the two?

In the middle of this conundrum, our class was visited by the District Head of the Social Studies Department. They stood impressed by how much the children understood our government, power, needs, and justice. They noted that while they worked independently, they engaged in academic discussions about fairness and justice. These children's wonderings had been honored and so their learning had deepened. I felt encouraged and faithful to give space for their research to blossom into children-created books, and through these books, the children would have increased empathy and an awakened desire to live in harmony with others and meet the requirements of the Representation Project.

Openness & Acceptance

Sometimes, a part of me sees behaviors like Nathan's and Leno's and wonders, "What no-good are they up to?" I make assumptions that trigger me, and I react. I do not stay open. But at the best of times, I set aside my needs for a minute, and move toward the child with acceptance.

One day in my classroom, we were amid giving each other written affirmations read out loud. After Yassa had read her affirmation of her classmate to Amri, she started to hand it to him. Another classmate, Netrin, intercepted it and began to scribble on the back. Giggles followed. I felt my temperature rising followed by the thought of how dare he! With my voice, I hurled from across the circle at Netrin. "No! That is NOT ok!" Immediately, his body tensed, his arms locked to his side, and he stared at the floor. Yassa started to explain. I assumed she was going to suggest it was no big deal. I cut her off. "It is not okay!" Well, so much for the affirmation circle. We all took a deep breath. Another student, Nisjut, reminded us that we had agreed not to touch other people's work; that got me immediately back to center. I asked, "Do we want to talk about it now?" Most, including Netrin, indicated no. They wanted to continue with their affirmations. We continued until everyone had received an affirmation. Netrin continued to stand there, while the rest settled into their work. What had I triggered? Clearly, I had short-circuited and triggered something in him. I knew I had publicly shamed him; in his stage of development being part of the herd was paramount. I had ousted him and he in turn did not want to talk to me. I was filled with regret.

At the end of class, he approached me to talk. The schedule said I had five minutes to get to my next class. I paused, moved down to his eye level, and listened. Yassa had been writing "your momma" as an insult on people's stuff the last few days. So, Netrin and company had decided that they would write back "*tu mamá*" – your momma in Spanish – back to her. Netrin had suspected that

Yassa had written "your momma" on her affirmation to Nisjut. Evidence proved she had. He decided to defend his friend by writing over the same thing back to her. She had not kept the agreement; he thought it fair to give her the same back. So, he too did not keep a part of the agreement to ask for what you need with kindness. I too had not kept the agreement. Instead, a domino effect took over. We agreed to come back to the conversation as a whole class the next time we gathered for a circle meeting. We would all be given the chance to say what happened, what we were feeling, what we were thinking, and what we needed. We would have an opportunity to share what we own, what we regret, and what we would do now having more insight. We would together affirm each other and share what we appreciate about each other. We would review what, if any, new agreements we needed to make around our 'oops!' and 'ouch!', terms I've adapted from Faith Bost (2020), Conscious Language facilitator and trainer, for actions that created pain points.

I have noticed that many of our conflicts stemmed from an 'oops!' or an 'ouch'. In this instance we had both. I had established a signal for these moments: a hand over the heart and saying 'oops' or 'ouch.' Anyone could use the signal: observer, student, teacher. In addition, we had a second gesture as a reminder about our agreements on how we would care for each other and our environment. The second signal was walking to the person breaking the agreement and placing your hand gently on their shoulder until you had eye contact from them. Once the gentle touch on the shoulder garnered eye contact, then you give them a positively framed reminder. For example, "Please use a lower voice." We also had a bell that our Bell Boss (a student) could ring to signal for a pause, redirection, transition, or silence (see Figure 5.7). We had a peace rose available to offer to someone with whom you wanted to resolve a conflict (see Figure 5.9). The children had been empowered to do all of these with each other, me included.

It was beautiful when the signals were used to remind me or anyone about an 'oops' or an 'ouch.' As for the children, the reverence and calm palpable in our space brought me much ease as an educator. Children moved with a feeling of empowerment and safety. Why had none of the signals been used in this case with me?

We also infused role-playing virtues in curricular lessons also assisted children in more practice in caring for each other and our space. For this reason, I fell in love with Montessori lessons which nurtured at once, the mind, heart, and hands of the child. A math Montessori lesson afforded me another moment to incorporate fairness, thoughtfulness, and such. For example, at the beginning of the division lesson, we give one (part of dividend) to each (divisor number) before anyone gets a second because we like to be fair. If there are any leftovers that cannot be shared equally, we set those aside (remainder). This role-playing and personification in elementary lessons had played a part in enticing the tendencies, and nurturing social virtues in the children; when was the last time I had incorporated these into the curriculum?

98 Spirituality in the Classroom – What Do the Teachers Say?

We gave Grace & Courtesy lessons in which the children received lessons on how to greet someone, how to welcome a visitor, how to ask for a turn, and how to resolve a conflict. Together in my elementary classes, we would role-play different approaches for the same conflict and decide which increased our connection with each other and honored our agreements. Sometimes, I initiated the lessons based on classroom conflicts I observed, and sometimes students brought forth a conflict they needed to be resolved (see Figure 5.8). Clearly, I needed to return and continue to repeat lessons!

FIGURE 5.7 Talking piece and bell

Source: Jennifer Mata-McMahon

FIGURE 5.8 Peace rose

Source: Jennifer Mata-McMahon

100 Spirituality in the Classroom – What Do the Teachers Say?

FIGURE 5.9 Grace and courtesy lesson

Source: Jennifer Mata-McMahon

Preparation as an Adult

Returning to that moment in our affirmation circle, I recognized that my mind's assumptions, my emotions, and my physical sensations all arose and guided my actions. Wanting to be efficient and "nip it in the bud" (it being Netrin's behavior

Vignettes From Ms. Escarfuller's Classroom **101**

and my discomfort), I missed the opportunity to model our agreement. Our agreement around nurturing each other's spirits and spirituality had been violated. How did we build connection and harmony again?

After school once at home, I sat in silence. That day, I had arrived at school with little sleep, an empty belly, and back-to-back classes and I had my attention fixed externally – on the children, the schedule, the emails. No prayers, no morning meditation, no positive self-affirmations, no breathwork. My Energy Codes Coach, Hui-Ling Singer, tells me, "Remember to keep one eye on the inside." She says, "Make sure your emotions and thoughts don't hijack your spirit's driving of the bus."

Thoughts of our peace area and our peace rose arose. I remembered the quiet space, deep belly breathing, and journaling. Many possibilities already existed in the classroom. I reminded myself to get back in the saddle and give it another go. I would give my students this compassionate encouragement. I would show faith in them. Having an honest conversation and holding myself accountable to repair would be a model for them on how to navigate their own 'oopsies!' and 'ouches!'.

I know my preparation directly connects to how everything will flow in my classroom. Performing my personal spiritual practice habits and nurturing those of the children in the classroom bubbled up as a priority. How do I create a space for and nurture these during the daily school schedule? Where do I (or the children) go to practice and exercise during the day or is spiritual practice regulated to my (and the children's) private time?

Listening for That Inner Voice

Together with some of my six- to nine-year-old children, we brainstormed about how to find our center again and listen to our inner wisdom. Together, we practiced deliberate breathing, for example, "Breathe in through your nose into your belly and blow it up like a balloon. Breathe out through your nose and send your breath out through the top of your head like a whale, pushing the air out by pushing your belly into your back flat as a pancake." Together, we grounded ourselves using our five senses, for example, we would silently say to ourselves "I smell one smell of . . . , I see two items that calm me . . . , I feel the seat supporting me . . . , I hear the whirring of the fan . . . , I taste the saltiness of my saliva . . ." We would do this at times of transition, and toward the beginning of class. Initially, we practiced sharing our sensations together. Then, we transitioned into holding that conversation 'in our head.'

For one class, we consistently started our first transition with group meditation time. They thought it might be helpful to "not get on each other's nerves so much." They agreed this would be a silent time. Those who preferred to silently read independently or to silently draw were permitted. Only those who volunteered to participate came to the meditation. Our bell signaled time

102 Spirituality in the Classroom – What Do the Teachers Say?

for whole class silence; students prepared and settled into whatever spot felt best: in a comfy chair, by a window, on the floor, or at a seat. I used sources from YouTube to find meditations with positive self-affirmations and breathing techniques. We started with one minute of silence, then three, then five, until eventually they would stay engaged in the silence for ten minutes; we did not practice further because of schedule constraints. The students, as did I, noticed they enjoyed this pause. By the end of our year together, most of the children had joined consistently; we were a community gathered in silent common purpose. Now, we were also approaching each other with more kindness and our work with more confidence.

Gratitude

Gratefulness is another regular centering practice we share in the classroom. Sometimes it comes in the form of modeling my turning to gratitude to get back to center; a student that triggers something in me may hear me say with genuine appreciation from me, "Thank you for that – you're my angel reminding me to grow in patience." At other times, it appears after a class conflict when I express gratitude for being able to turn to each other in faith and with responsibility for each other; I feel grateful for our improved skills and our stronger connection.

I have also carved time in our day, to express gratitude at the beginning and end of class. The child chosen as Bell Boss rings our small class bell and leads the gratitude time. The Capturing Kids Heart (CKH) training by the Flippen Group has a similar beginning called "good things" (Flippen, 2022). From this training, I now consciously encourage the Bell Boss to ask two follow-up questions after each child has shared what they are grateful for, to model caring to the speaker. In addition, I learned to monitor the time, from three to five minutes, to stay efficient within my block of time with the children.

The children share gratefulness, for family members, friends, teachers, pets, playing with someone, and learning new things. During this time, I invite the children to listen to the gratitude and to give a thumb-up signal or a wave if they agree. Each of the children sharing their gratitude is invited to look around and notice how many other friends share the same gratitude. After our shared gratitudes, I invite them to notice how they feel inside thinking of all those gratitudes and encourage them to continue sharing their gratitudes with someone throughout their day and to recall them during challenging moments. We usually have a talking piece, a Japanese wooden doll (see Figure 5.7) or a soft palm-sized stuffed doll, to practice fair turn taking too.

Turning to nature, we share gratefulness for the sun making all of life possible, for the oxygen from the ocean, drinking water on a hot day. When we do gather to share a meal, we sing a thank you to the sun, the earth, the water,

Vignettes From Ms. Escarfuller's Classroom   **103**

and the plants for the gifts we are about to eat. We pause to acknowledge the abundance before us, dependent of the effort of Nature and other humans, most unseen to us.

Finding Meaning – A Montessori Great Lesson: The Story of The Coming of the Universe

Believing that we are part of an interdependent connected Cosmos, of something greater than ourselves that we call Spirit, necessitates from me a choice, either to act with the flow of Spirit's actions or to learn through the resulting friction of human-guided actions, and "the feedback loop," explained in Chapter 4. I consciously choose to seek a greater understanding of this interconnectedness, why it exists, and how it came to be.

Am I too old to be giddy at the sight of the first tulip of spring? Is the child too young to wonder about how the Universe came into form? Dr. Maria Montessori created what she called "The Great Lessons." Every year, the six- to 12-year-old children receive these Great Lessons; they are primarily given to the six- to nine-year-old group. I perceive that these lessons line the entirety of the elementary curriculum with spirituality, or the essence of who we are. These lessons are like a scaffolding of natural laws to guide the children, and me, in our natural development toward harmony with ourselves and others. They invite the children to wonder about creation, the order of the Universe, laws, and fundamental truths. They invite the children to safely explore the mysteries that lie therein. They flame the children's imagination and help them orient themselves in the Cosmos. As such, they give me as the guide and the children a secure reference point for keeping the focus on developing our spirituality, our Highest Self, while engaged in our curricular endeavors.

The first lesson, The Coming of the Universe, holds a special place in my heart; it gives the children a compassionate compass on which to contextualize all their learning. Told like around the campfire, the story unfolds through demonstrations, experiments, and illustrations, into awed enthusiasm. The story gifts the child a picture of the natural order and laws of everything in the Cosmos. Everything has work to do and rules to follow. Everything has a purpose and value in the Universe. Everything grows and changes. Everything exists as interdependent and connected. Every problem has a solution, creating something new; nothing lost or wasted.[3] After this story, the children require a pause. The children begin to share their wonder. Who/What created the Universe? Why was it all created? Usually, much conversation ensues. Then the word comes up. God. Every year, I have anticipated their definitions with relish. The following photos come from several different classes of an approximate total of 75, six- to seven-year-old students, after hearing the Story of the Universe. Most of their definitions fell into one of six categories: God as Creator above us, God as Creator among us, God as

FIGURE 5.10   God as Protector, from Evil

Source: Patricia Escarfuller

Protector, God as Provider, God as Judge of punishment/reward, God as Nature (see Figures 5.10–5.18).

The children who drew God as above us understood that 'he' never died.[4] This God above us "wrapped you in a big hug" and gave us all that was good. For some, this God also "fought all the bad spirits" away from Earth, while clearly above us. As six-year-old Maria explained, having heard the Story of The Coming of the Universe, "God saves me from the devil, because the devil is bad. And the devil tortures you. And that is evil. God can do anything for you." For others, God was part of everyday life, found in the rivers, trees, or your walk to/from school. God was felt through the senses and seen in a rainbow, the smell of a flower, the cuddling with a pet. God helped you feel better. God made all things. Maria added, "My mom made me. My grandmom made my mom. Grandmom was the first mom. God made the first mom."

Some children saw God primarily as a judge of whether you deserved punishment or reward, of whether you were 'Good' or 'Bad'. Ramya, age six, explained. "I lied. And he punished me." "How did he punish you?", I asked. "My parents got mad at me. They didn't let me play with my dog." Several children mentioned

Vignettes From Ms. Escarfuller's Classroom **105**

FIGURE 5.11 God as Protector, with Hug

Source: Patricia Escarfuller

lying as a major offense to God. Lying to avoid punishment would probably result in harsher consequences from God. One boy confidently stated, "It is what, not who!" The same boy also concurred there was evil. He shared, "I broke into hell. The couches are made of human flesh. I saw skeletons. Hell is there so people who do bad things can be punished when they die. Your spirit is being tortured." When asked to define spirit he replied without hesitation. "Spirits are light projected by death. Spirits are a type of light. Spirits are made of memories and standing outside of me." Many depicted the cross, reflecting the Christian background of most of the children (see Figure 5.17). They shared that God had come down as Jesus to protect us. Sadrit, age seven, shared that God had died as Jesus to give us blood to live.

Even though there were different perspectives, all perspectives were acknowledged by the children. That discussion laid a foundation for establishing care for each other and for wondering about our connection to something greater than

106 Spirituality in the Classroom – What Do the Teachers Say?

FIGURE 5.12 God Creator Among Us

Source: Patricia Escarfuller

FIGURE 5.13 God Creator Above Us

Source: Patricia Escarfuller

FIGURE 5.14 God as Nature

Source: Patricia Escarfuller

ourselves. Creating a space to give the Story of The Coming of the Universe and then listen to the stories they already held to explain how and why the Universe came to be permitted them to explore and validated this aspect of themselves that searches for meaning. In the feverish engagement of the hands in their Creation drawing, in the attentive ears and eyes listening to their classmates' stories, and in the loquacious flow of ideas lay a nurturance of spirituality.

Some common threads arose from their discussions, drawings, and stories. The Universe is real. There is some invisible force orchestrating all of existence. There are rules to follow. Something created all of this. There is goodness. There is happiness and security. There is sadness and fear. Evil was equivalent to suffering and pain. From a young age, the children were aware on some level that something beyond human experience was at play.

108 Spirituality in the Classroom – What Do the Teachers Say?

FIGURE 5.15 God as Judge

Source: Patricia Escarfuller

FIGURE 5.16 God as Provider

Source: Patricia Escarfuller

Emotional Awareness

Of all these threads, I was curious about their belief about the origin of emotions. How did the sadness, happiness, fear, and security get in you? One boy shared, "Feelings were invented by inventors . . . pause . . . many years ago.

FIGURE 5.17 God on the Cross

Source: Patricia Escarfuller

They (inventors) are not around anymore." Some children agreed with another male peer who shared, "God made us and put emotions in us." A female peer shared, "God gave us those emotions so we could have fun, because he also gave us sadness." She felt there was a balance between good and evil. Others found a connection to God through emotions. Aleria shared, "We have all these emotions because God feels these emotions and so we do as well." Some did say that others put these emotions in them when they bother them. When asked how some shared, they come through the eyes. Others shared that they just show up. A few said that the mom gives you these emotions while you're a baby in her. One six-year-old girl, who had drawn a sad God with a question mark overhead surrounded by a rainbow, "Why does God get annoyed if he can do something [about it]?"

Emotions show up in each moment of our lives, at all ages, and wherever we travel. They are tools we carry to communicate whether we're on course and centered or veering off the road. They are the highway treads to make sure we

110 Spirituality in the Classroom – What Do the Teachers Say?

stay 'on the road'. For me, emotion is a form of communication for your spirit; it points to a need to be met or a belief to be considered. Sometimes, however, I understand we identify as being the emotion that arises in us; sometimes I forget that I am bigger than it. I know my children do and I reassure them that identifying as the emotion happens to many of us.

So how do we use our understanding of emotions to aid our developing spirituality?

For my group of approximately 27 first graders in the traditional setting, this beginning of class time involved a wheel of emotions. Four questions were asked in order: (1) What emotions do we feel now?, (2) Where do you feel this emotion in your body?, (3) What brought this emotion up in you?, and (4) How do you want to care for this emotion?

Each group of emotions was represented by a number and a visual of a face expressing that emotion. After the striking of the bell for silence, and our greeting song, I would ask, "What emotions do we feel now?" The slide with the visual of the emotion wheel could be seen by everyone. I would call on three students at most. Children would raise their hands signaling the number that corresponded to their emotion. I was the reporter interviewing live from the classroom about what emotions we were experiencing today, and I had a pretend microphone to interview the chosen volunteer. I would put a lookout hand to my forehead and scan the room. Sometimes, I selected a child who represented the majority of how the rest of the group was feeling. In this way, we could give space to the emotions that filled the room. Sometimes, I selected the child that represented the least felt emotion in the group. Here, the goal was for the child to be accompanied, understood, and acknowledged. Initially, we focused on identifying and naming our feelings. The children were quick to name scared, sad, happy, or mad. I started from there. After about four weeks of implementing this strategy three times a week, the children were using more varied language. Happy could now be excited, energized content. Sad was lonely, disappointed, or heartbroken. Disappointed came up a lot; I noticed many times it was around adults not following through on promises.

The one emotion that was never coming up was anger. I felt stumped. With vividness, I remember Dr. Mata's encouraging suggestions on how to dig into this phenomenon. The next time I met with the class, I reserved some time to ask if anyone ever felt angry. I gave an example of when I have anger bubbling up in me. "Sometimes I feel angry when I think something is not fair. Sometimes I feel angry when I don't get my way." The boys shared first. They felt angry when they lost a soccer game. They felt angry when someone hurt them on purpose. They felt angry when they were not allowed to join a game. All the children validated with a clap or snap at least one of these examples. Then I asked, "Is it okay to feel angry?" Lunging forward came a booming "NO!" Feeling angry was definitely

Vignettes From Ms. Escarfuller's Classroom **111**

'not okay'. Feeling angry was 'bad'. I wondered, are there other feelings that are not okay? The children identified all the 'negative' emotions (which come from unmet needs according to the founder of Non-Violent Communication, Marshall Rosenberg) as being bad and not okay. They knew they were bad because they hurt. They knew they were bad because they were punished for them.

How did I accurately and gently convey my belief that all their emotions were okay? Was it my responsibility to do so? How did I respond while modeling acceptance for their point of view? An inspired idea entered my mind. What if they are okay simply because they are? What if what is not okay is hurting other people when you feel these things? The room was silent. We decided that we would just wonder about it for that day.

Eventually in the subsequent weeks, we wondered if these emotions were telling us something. We wondered when exactly anger shows up. How about fear and sadness? Together, the children began to connect that these occurred when they didn't get what they needed. We decided all these 'negative' emotions were okay; we did not agree on how they got in us in the first place. We went through each category of emotions and reminded ourselves that these were all important and okay. We did agree that hurting people, animals, trees, or things, because of these feelings, was not okay. We practiced naming fear. We practiced identifying the need behind fear. We thanked fear for helping us know what we needed. And we hugged ourselves. We repeated this exercise over and over for several negative emotions. After four months, and as children refined their knowledge, we would each hug ourselves and add verbally, "All my emotions are okay."

My follow-up question was, "Where do you feel it in your body?" The children found their feelings in their bellies, hands, and feet mostly. The feet wanted to move, the hands wanted to hug, clench, or throw, and the bellies wanted to tumble and rumble. Surprisingly, they easily identified what their body wanted to do or felt; I needed more time to locate where I was feeling certain emotions in my body. Then I asked, "What happened to bring up that emotion in you?" The children shared a range of experiences; most were around gifts, appreciation, celebrations, loss, friendships, family, and conflicts.

Like the first question, the final question, "How do you want to care for that emotion?" took some teasing out. Children initially volunteered just a few answers: get a hug, play, or be left alone. Here too, I thought I would dig a little bit deeper. The children now had a more nuanced emotional vocabulary, accepted that all emotions are okay, and validated each other's experiences. Now, they were invited to consider additional ways they could soothe themselves. Eventually, their answers grew from three to more than nine different ways of soothing their emotions. I could see and feel their pride in their discovery. Then the school year ended. What would happen if we could have continued to build upon our

112 Spirituality in the Classroom – What Do the Teachers Say?

discoveries? What would happen if we were together for three or more years in a row as in a Montessori classroom?

I believe some of the beauty of this emotional exercise came from the validation the children received. For each question, we would ask for a hand wave or snap from anyone that also had a similar answer. Children would look around to identify who shared in their experience. They felt accompanied and connected. We would end by each of us giving ourselves a hug.

This entire exercise, from first question to last would take about five to eight minutes. By giving attention to these emotions, the children were gaining skills, as I was, in the regular practice of naming, locating, sensing, and caring for their emotions. They learned to embrace them instead of rejecting them. More and more, they could find the need behind the emotion, whether a positive or negative emotion. The children would speak from a place of awareness, sharing the workings of their mind (thoughts), heart (emotions), and body (sensations).

My teacher trainings did not cover territory around the emotional self; no explicit instruction around emotional management as the adult in the classroom was given. My own regrets, curiosity around the purpose of suffering, and desire to heal from my personal traumas have motivated me to learn. With an expanded emotional language and skill set, after taking several workshops and courses, my feelings and thoughts still have the opportunity to flood me and hijack my actions. Then when I re-center and calm down, regret rises in me. So how overwhelming might the emotional world be to children without the language to name their emotions? How could they have power over what they did not understand about themselves?

Connection With Others: Friendship

One year in my second-grade classroom, a male child, D'Aleni was the center of many conflicts, conflicts that seemed to threaten the emotional and physical safety of the classroom. At home, my teenage children were trying to communicate their needs; resentment and retaliation on both sides were building. I did not get them. Their expression triggered many emotions in me, emotions I did not want to embrace but fix. I did more research. I listened to Ted Talks on YouTube. During one of my Ted Talk binges, I discovered Conscious Parenting Revolution by Katherine Winter-Sellery (YouTube, 2020). I was hooked immediately, plopped down a few grand, and took her online course. Here she outlined step-by-step actions, and accompanying language, for nurturing the spirituality of the child. Like Dr. Maria Montessori, she presented the child as a whole and completely valuable entity, inherently worthy of attention, appreciation, and admiration. Having trained directly with Marshall Rosenberg in Non-Violent Communication, she

Vignettes From Ms. Escarfuller's Classroom **113**

created a clear picture of the link between our thoughts, emotions, actions, and our needs. I thought I was ready. Then she introduced me to this quote:

The ability to observe without evaluating is the highest form of intelligence.
~ *Indian philosopher Jiddu Krishnamurti*

Aha! That is exactly what Montessori meant in the observation of the child! I was full of judgments and accusations. I had to take a step back to observe D'Aleni, and my own children, without judgment. Deep breath. It required me to empathize with and embrace all ranges of emotion, thought, sensation, and manifestation with reverence and free of judgment. Could I see each moment as potential to manifest a greater harmony, flow, ease, and love with everything and everyone around me? After all, this interdependent harmony defined spirituality for me too. For me, I stated that the aim of education was to nurture the spirit of the child toward his innately driven work; in working this way the child is a new beginning moving us toward a more harmonious interdependence. In the classroom, learning literacy, mathematics, and so forth would flow from feeding the tendencies of the child at each developmental stage. So, any skills taught are scaffolded by a nurturance of spirituality. Except how could I do this when I was so full of judgment?

I would just give it my best effort. My classroom would be a 'fault-shame-guilt-blame-free' zone. When a conflict arises, I would remember to accept that everybody involved and surrounding the event (including me as a guide) is impacted. Therefore, the conflict is an opportunity revealed for everyone. It is an opportunity to translate the language of the body, mind, and heart into the language of needs. Did I have faith that the 'tragic expressions of unmet needs' surrounding these highly charged emotions and sensations would resolve when I moved from judging these actions to embracing, and empathizing with them? My opportunity would come soon enough. I remember one like it was yesterday. D'Aleni gets angry and throws the Legos on the floor during indoor recess. I hear, "Stop calling me a thief! I didn't steal your piece! I had it all the time!" The other children don't believe him. George comes to tell me that D'Aleni threw the Legos on the floor and is yelling at people. Everyone else continues with their play; I know their ears are perked up. D'Aleni is sitting in a corner balled up, head tucked in and arms around his legs. I respond to George. Adapting language from Katherine Winter-Sellery's training, I begin:

"Is everybody safe?"
George: "Yes"
Me: "It looks like anger got inside of D'Aleni."
George: "Yes"
Me: "I wonder what his anger is all about. I wonder what his need is?"
George: "We don't know, but he took our Lego! And he's yelling at us!"

114 Spirituality in the Classroom – What Do the Teachers Say?

Me: "So, it sounds like you got filled with frustration at D'Aleni's actions, yes?"

George: "YES!"

Me: "Because you want to count on having the pieces you need?"

George: "Yes"

Me: "And you need the Lego pieces to be shared fairly?"

George: "Yes"

Me: "And you need for D'Aleni to speak to you in a quieter voice?"

George: "Yes"

Me: "You feel safer when he speaks to you in a regular voice?"

George: "Yes"

Me: "Hmm, I wonder what D'Aleni needs. Would you be willing to ask him?"

George: "No. And he doesn't want to talk to us right now.

Me: "Hmmm, I see that. He's taking care of the anger that got inside him. Please give him space to take care of his anger. We can invite him to talk when he is ready."

George: "Ok"

Me: "Would you be willing to also pause on your play with Legos?"

George: "No"

Me: "Would you be willing to play with just the pieces you have for now?"

George: "Ok"

Me: "Thank you for your patience and giving D'Aleni space. We'll come back together when we're all ready to talk about what we need."

Eventually, we were able to gather, and the boys took turns hearing each other out. My role was to guide and remind them, by modeling, that our classroom was a judgment-free zone (our aim) and we choose to care for each other and to ask for what we needed with kindness; everybody matters. The boys decided that at the end of the day all the Lego pieces needed to be returned to the bin, no saving pieces for the next day.[5] Being able to create a small space to listen created an opportunity for the boys to find connection. With each connection, D'Aleni got down to the business of acquiring curricular knowledge and skills for a longer period. D'Aleni continued to develop his skills.

About two months later, the tables were turned. George had torn up D'Aleni's paper. D'Aleni approached me distraught, tears steadily running down his cheeks. "I don't know what got in him! I was just working, and he crumbled up my paper!" I focused on validating the feelings and the needs behind his tears; he needed George to be nice to him. D'Aleni decided he could approach George directly.

D'Aleni: "You crumbled my paper? You feeling angry?"

George: "Yes!"

D'Aleni: "Why?"

George: "You took away my best friend [Yory]!" (I guided him naming his emotions and needs; he felt fear around not having anyone with whom to play and needed to belong)

Vignettes From Ms. Escarfuller's Classroom **115**

D'Aleni: "I want to be his friend too. How about we all three work together?"

George: "No." (here D'Aleni shared he felt sad because he liked working with Yory too)

D'Aleni: "Why not?"

George: "Because you do everything better than me!"

The buzz of the rest of the classroom at work was silenced. All energy was on this dialogue.

I interjected, "George, do you feel jealousy?" Yes. George nodded, and tears streamed down his cheeks.

(Pause)

D'Aleni gave him a hug.

D'Aleni responded, "You probably feel bad about yourself. Sometimes I feel bad about my work too. But I try my best and I keep practicing. And sometimes you do things better than me."

George looked up.

Others came up to hug George. Others hugged both.

D'Aleni: "How about the three of us do the work together?"

This time George agreed.

Previously, this interaction may have gone more like this: I would see the behavior, the crumbled paper. I would give my best stare, aghast. I would state righteously that is not how we agreed to treat each other. I would ask the child how he/she was going to make it better. I would do everything in my power to make him make it better. I would call home. I would have him redo D'Aleni's work for homework. I would have them sit far apart from each other. I would make George sit close to me. Thankfully, none of this happened.

That day instead, D'Aleni's confidence and empathy for others grew. From that moment, more children were asking, "What feeling do you have now?" "What do you need?" "What feeling got in you?" They began to demonstrate greater care and self-management and asserting themselves more. Fault, shame, guilt, and blame slowly transformed into curiosity, understanding, acceptance, and faith.

This new way of seeing behavior seemed familiar on some level. The speedy steps and language, modeled earlier, for getting to these emotions and needs driving those 'tragic expressions', as Winter-Sellery calls them, were the new tools I needed. Many persistent behavioral issues slowly dissolved into properly expressed emotions, across the many grade levels I was teaching at that time (K-5th grades). Imagine what might manifest in our schools if each time there was a conflict or a 'tragic expression', and we:

1. saw the child tossing anger, sadness, fear, judgment is having an expression (perhaps a belief, a judgment, a memory) attached to an unmet need;
2. noticed our own feelings, thoughts, memories, and unmet needs simultaneously surfacing;

116 Spirituality in the Classroom – What Do the Teachers Say?

3. remembered, as Faith Bost shares in her Conscious Language trainings, that our feeling/emotion world speaks as honestly as a two- to three-year-old would, and therefore;
4. we created a gap to observe and listen to what was arising for the child; and
5. responded to the thoughts of the other and our 'inner child' with the same gentle care we'd give to a two- to three-year-old child.

How do I carve time in a schedule overflowing with commitments, meetings, and classes to role-play or brainstorm different scenarios with my colleagues in which to practice these skills? How do I strengthen my resolve to receive with reverence 'tragic expressions of unmet needs?' How do I receive professional training around practices like these that nurture a child's spiritual development, his/her willingness to manifest through his work? How often would we practice in order to gain mastery?

Inner Peace

I applied these techniques of identifying thoughts, emotions, and needs behind behaviors with one of my five-year-old children named Clarence. Every time I walked into class, I found him crying uncontrollably. I knew from my Montessori training to provide a consistent structure for this age group, same routines on different days. I acknowledged the tears with a nod, a tissue, and a permitted holding of hands, as I continued with the routines and lesson for the 45-minute block: greetings, gratitude, singing together, reading together, presentation of lesson, activity/work (I have a turn, you have a turn), observation, clean up, gather, share outs, leave with a smile, and warm wishes. Each time we got to the lesson part the crying got louder. He screamed, "I can't do it! Help me!" I would give the lesson again and offer him a turn next. "I can't!" And he began to inch closer to me until he came to sit right next to me for each class. The tears deafened any other sound. Still, I saw progress in his moving toward me.

Winter-Sellery et al. (2022) offered that perhaps he thought his work needed to look just like mine, perhaps it needed to be his vision of perfect, perhaps it needed to look like someone else's work. How about focusing on self-growth and self-expression instead? Help the children to look inwardly, to be self-referenced. Ah, yes! I was still trying to fix the emotion rather than meet the need. The next time, at a share-out time, I offered, "Look how we all received the same instruction, and they all came out so differently! How fun!" We celebrated everyone's work. Clarence was still crying, albeit a little less. In the following class, I offered, "how about we try building our paper sculptures again?" "How about we see how much we've grown?" Sitting next to me he practiced on his own; I remained silent. We did this for two more classes with slight variations for each class; everyone could use the practice.

Eventually, he had a paper sculpture monster that included the required pleats, folds, rolls of paper, as well as the triangle, circle, and square cutouts. He exclaimed, "I did it!" I responded with a smile, "Congratulations! You did it!" After that, he settled. I remembered to present projects that would build on his skills, and to also signal to him when we would have something totally new; witnessing his increasingly quiet attention at lessons I perceived he began to feel less frightened of new projects. Eventually, he no longer needed to sit next to me and found another peer to imitate instead. With his spirit at peace, he moved his attention to his work with a focus on self-evaluation. How do I consistently support children to stay self-referenced when surrounded by rewards and punishments (aka consequences)?

Connection With Nature: Our Environment

As seen earlier, most of our thoughts and emotions seem to surface through the sensorial experiences in our environment. For example, the smell of coffee embraces me with loving memories of warm summer days sitting under a soursop tree with my aunt while we swapped stories and news. What stimulating sensorial experiences do we give our children that support their natural tendencies, their inner urgings? How do we simultaneously plan for soothing sensorial experiences to center us spiritually? How do we give them more positive sensorial experiences to outweigh the negative experiences with which they come to the classroom?

Just like the preparation of the adult, Maria Montessori urges us to prepare the environment with much intentionality and purpose for each material and its placement,

> to prepare a 'suitable environment' just as we should place a branch of a tree in an aviary . . . the surrounding objects should be proportioned to the size and strength of the child . . . the field thus opened to the free activity of the child will enable him to exercise himself as a man. It is not movement for its own sake that he will derive from these exercises, but a powerful coefficient in the complex formation of his personality.
>
> (Montessori, 1991, p. 118)

What will the child smell when she walks in? What tactile materials would entice her to work? What does she see? What is in her vantage point? What does she hear? The outdoors seems to be a ripe environment to entice and to challenge the child. In this way, the child is in direct contact with the Universe. All the senses are awakened in nature and thus the child may reveal herself more.

One afternoon, I took my first graders outside to work. Having practiced some observational drawing indoors of pencils, vases, and such, we were now

118 Spirituality in the Classroom – What Do the Teachers Say?

aiming to draw directly from nature, specifically leaves. Fortunately, our school has a massive yard filled with a fruit orchard, garden beds, perennial shrubs, and grassy fields. The children brought their clipboards, pencils, and paper. We gathered around a giant oak and reviewed what we had agreed to do to keep us safe and to complete our mission. Then off they went to gather a leaf that enticed them to illustrate it. As they searched, I observed Ariel being followed by six other girls; she was like the Mother Hen guiding her chicks. In the indoor classroom arrangement, it may have taken me a long time to discover this unspoken hierarchy, and intrinsic ability. Now I had identified a leader among the girls in a matter of minutes. The same happened with the boys. Two boys that never were near each other in class started 'planning' together. Where they up to mischief? No, they were devising a plan for finding the biggest leaf in the area; one would look around the trees and the other one would walk up and down the grassy field. Another boy, Tony, normally quiet inside, swaggered confidently outside and invited boys over to his spot to collect 'cool leaves'. The boys listened to him. He was our supporter. That day, the boys seemed gentler with each other outside than inside; pencil poking was replaced with an intense shared curiosity around bugs. The girls were busy organizing their leaves by size. In minutes, I discovered their attraction to certain life in nature, their attraction toward each other or not, and their physical strengths. Through their purposeful movements in nature, they were building connections with each other and their natural world.

Our outdoor environment also provided opportunities to collaborate across grades and content. One year, our first through fifth-grade classes took on our first Tulip Project, with the help of Mr. Akil Rahim, founder of The George Washington Carver DISCO STEAM Inverturers, who was part of the National Tulip Citizen Project. The fifth-grade children organized and gathered all the materials and prepared the soil; they divided the tulips into sets of ten and loosened the hardened soil. The second and third graders excavated holes for the younger children to place their bulbs. The fourth graders potted a group of tulips on the balcony to compare with the planted garden tulips. The children's work had practical real-world value and purpose; they made posters, planted tulips, and worked to help someone else. All the children engaged in measuring, documenting, researching, writing, and illustrating, and then waited (see Figure 5.18).

Children eagerly anticipated the arrival of the tulips in Spring; who would see them first and where? Upon their discovery of the first blossom, a few children ran inside to share the news; over the intercom, the office staff excitedly declared the welcome of the red beauty! Many months later, this singular tulip's announcement revealed the children's joy in their work, their connectedness with each other, and their new appreciation of the natural world.

May these vignettes inspire hope for our work with children. May they also encourage us to dialogue more around best practices for nurturing children's

Vignettes From Ms. Escarfuller's Classroom   119

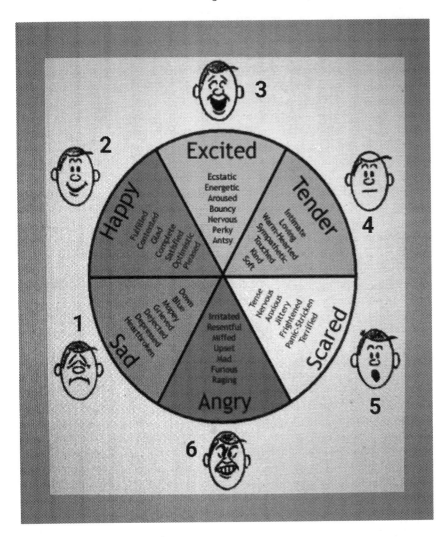

FIGURE 5.18   Emotion wheel

Source: Patricia Escarfuller

spirituality. "An education capable of saving humanity is no small undertaking; it involves the spiritual development of man, the enhancement of his value as an individual, and the preparation of young people to understand the times in which they live" (Montessori, 2015, p. 34). To do it well, it takes administrators, trainers, families, community members, and inspired leaders working together to raise a new village.

FIGURE 5.19 Tulip Project work

Source: Patricia Escarfuller

Notes

1. To learn about Title 1 schools in the U.S. visit the U.S. Department of Education website https://www2.ed.gov/programs/titleiparta/index.html
2. Tracing the trade journey of the fabric used, measuring the fabric, creating the pillow shape, and creating a repeated pattern with the stitching.
3. My spiritual lens and my understanding of current quantum physics, the concept that everything lives as energy, is also added to and lies within this story.

4. One female child explained, "God is not a girl. He is a boy. I saw him in church." – other children agreed.
5. This was later modified for big projects, but for the most part, any loose pieces were to be put back in the bin.

References

Bost, F. (2020). *Conscious language workshop*. Retrieved November 1, 2022, from https://faithinwellness.com/

Flippen, F. (2022). *Capturing kid's hearts*. Retrieved November 1, 2022, from www.capturingkidshearts.org/

Montessori, M. (1991). *The advanced Montessori method* (Vol. 1, pp. 117–118). Clio Press.

Montessori, M. (2015). *Education and peace* (The Montessori Series, Vol. 10, p. 34). Montessori-Pierson Publishing Company

Winter-Sellery, K., Porter, L., & Jamieson, C. N. (2022). *Conscious parenting revolution course*. Retrieved November 1, 2022, from https://consciousparentingrevolution.com/

YouTube. (2020, February 13). From overriding my inner knowing and to trusting myself [Video]. *YouTube*. www.ted.com/talks/katherine_winter_sellery_from_overriding_my_inner_knowing_to_trusting_myself

SECTION III

Tying It All Together

In this, the third and closing section of the book, theory and practice are connected in order to bridge the theoretical framework and the research findings mentioned in Section I, with the classroom vignettes and photos presented in Section II, in order to offer a clear path forward in including spirituality in secular public educational spaces. Chapter 6 presents a brief explanation of the establishment and the free exercise clauses of the U.S. Constitution to make the case for spiritual nourishment in public spaces, a justification and advocacy for holistic views of development, and a review of the literature and research regarding nurturing and supporting spiritual development in the classroom. Guidelines are provided, for intentionally nurturing spirituality in secular public educational settings. A focus on an intentional (yet hidden) curriculum approach is offered, demonstrating how nurturing children's spirituality can be achieved by opening spaces to explore *the big questions* and supporting spiritual moments with children (and not necessarily exclusively by embracing faith-based curricula). Chapter 7 introduces the proposition of spirituality as the North Star for education and explains how teacher education programs can be the starting point in order to center the educational experience as a holistic experience, focused on the spirit. This chapter explores initiatives in teacher preparation programs to prepare educators to understand the child from a holistic framework, which includes supporting and nurturing spirituality as part of their role as curriculum developers and instructors of academic skills and knowledge, as well as educators of the whole child with the goal of facilitating their development as integrally complex and layered human beings.

DOI: 10.4324/9781003081463-9

6

HOW CAN WE NURTURE CHILDREN'S SPIRITUALITY IN SECULAR SETTINGS?

When my nephew, Nick, was around 6 years old, he asked me "Je Ji," – my niece and nephew call me Je Ji – "Je Ji, is God real?" I paused and thought to myself, "Now this has got to be a teachable moment if there ever was one!"

Yet, I also knew that whatever I answered could potentially influence his beliefs and certainly color his faith. So, in true Piagetian fashion, I did what any constructivist teacher worth her salt would have done, I redirected the question and said, "That's a really good question Nick, what do you think?" He thought for a moment and answered, "I think God is real, but not real like a house. I think he is real like love." I smiled, and repeated, "God is real like love." Nick is now all grown up and recently graduated from Carnegie Mellon University with a degree in Statistics and Machine Learning, and currently believes, "God made the universe as a really big terrarium, and once put in motion, God '*peaced*' out and is just content watching everything grow and develop" (Sanderson, electronic communication, September 15, 2022).

Now, it seems like Nick's understanding of God has changed and morphed through the years, yet it began at a young age with a pondering that resulted in a question to an adult he trusted. It is because of these questions that children ponder, questions so powerful and so important in determining how they understand the world around them as well as themselves as human beings, questions that ultimately shape the adults they will become, that I believe it is of utmost importance to nurture, alongside with the body and the mind, the spirit of the child. Because of questions like this one, and the way in which it was mediated, that allowed for him to come to his own answer, Nick advanced in his spiritual development guided by a belief in a God that is real like love, meaning it can't be seen or touched, but it certainly can be perceived and experienced.

DOI: 10.4324/9781003081463-10

126 Tying It All Together

Later, as an adult, his understanding evolved into a definition that better reflects his lived experiences.

During that teachable moment, when Nick was six years old, I was able to mediate his understanding due to my preparation as a constructivist educator; an educator who sets the stage for children to uncover and construct knowledge for themselves. Yet it was also because of my own prior experiences asking questions like this one when I was around six years old myself. I also had a caring and wise adult, my grandmother, who did the same for me, mediating my understanding of the world and allowing me to uncover its meaning and my purpose in it. I believe all children need to have this in their lives and I know teachers can do this for their young students if they allow for spaces to have these conversations and for children to develop enough trust in them to share their ponderings while trying to make sense of the world around them.

I would like for all teachers to be able to foster children on their own, unique spiritual paths, supporting them in uncovering and remembering why they are here and how to best participate in what we call life. Teachers can do this by not proselytizing one particular faith belief or providing absolutes when engaging with children's questions but by allowing them to discover the answer that best resonates with them. The belief and knowing that early childhood educators are in a privileged position to nurture children's spiritual selves in an authentic and responsible way is one of the drivers for the work I engage in. Yet this belief is not enough. In order for teachers to be able to nurture children in this aspect of their development, teachers need to be assured that they can legally do this and be taught how to do it without imposing their personal beliefs in order to facilitate it responsibly in the classroom, particularly in spaces that are secular and traditionally steer away from any spiritually focused pedagogies.

Understanding Our Constitutional Constraints

Childhood is a unique stage in a human being's life. It is a stage in which we are in a heightened learning state, everything is new and interesting, and we are primed to take it all in, and to learn using all our senses (Montessori, 1912; Snyder, 2014). However, school, as the quintessential location for teaching and for promoting learning for young students, is not always the most welcoming environment for this type of hands-on, sensory-based learning to occur. The goal of schooling has changed over time, moving from promoting critical thinking for the practice of freedom and the transformation of structures of oppression, to a focus on the integration of pupils into existing societal structures. This change encompasses what Paolo Freire called the banking concept of education, in which "the scope of action allowed to students extends only as far as receiving, filing, and storing the deposits" (Freire, 1997, p. 53), turning knowledge into a gift bestowed by those who consider themselves knowledgeable upon those whom they consider to know nothing (Freire, 1997). Because of historical events such as the Industrial Revolution, the launch of Sputnik, and more recently in the digital era, the Information Revolution, education has been forced to change its focus to teaching skills and testing for their acquisition (Palmer, 2003), preparing students for work environments that in the best of cases will advance society's standing in the world, if not merely preserve the ever declining status quo. This deviation from education's original aim has been to the detriment of a possible focus on developing holistic human beings, ones with solid skills in literacy and math, as well as a resilient moral compass and a strong connection to their true essence, in order to gain a clear understanding of life's meaning and their particular purpose of being within it (Palmer, 1993).

In the U.S., I believe some of this shift in the purpose of education, particularly in public education, is due to the misunderstanding of the establishment and the free exercise clauses presented in the constitution. The first amendment to the U.S. Constitution states, "Congress shall make no law respecting an establishment of religion or prohibiting the free exercise thereof" (National Archives, 2018), encompassing both what is known as the *establishment clause* and the *free exercise clause*. The common understanding of this portion of the first amendment of the U.S. Constitution referred to as the separation of church and state is limited to the establishment clause, by which proselytizing is not permitted in public settings funded by federal and/or state funds, such as public schools. Yet, if comprehensively understood including the free exercise clause, the separation of church and state alerts that prohibiting the free exercise of religious beliefs, and by direct association, of spiritual beliefs, should also not be enacted. Carpenter (2003) reminds us, "we should remember that not only do the courts forbid any action by government schools not prompted by a 'secular primary purpose' or which would 'principally and primarily' aid religion; they also forbid any that would *inhibit* it" (p. 44). A more comprehensive interpretation of these clauses opens the possibility to not only entertain different religious faiths and spiritual beliefs in public school classrooms but also understand spirituality as a broader phenomenon, different than one confined by a specific religion, as explained in Chapter 1.

A comprehensive and more accurate interpretation of the establishment and the free exercise clauses, accompanied by the understanding that spirituality is much broader and inclusive than any given religion, would allow for the consideration of the possibility of nurturing children's spirituality in public education without the worries of angry parents knocking on our classroom doors with concerns of proselytization. Or at least, would provide educators with solid arguments to support their decision to entertain, support, and nurture, children's spirituality in the classroom. With this newfound understanding of the separation of church and state, I would pose that all educators can and should make the consideration

128 Tying It All Together

to embrace this important and much-needed role. We could do so by emulating Parker Palmer's (2003) approach, he gracefully explains it as,

> I am no fan of state-sanctioned religions, or of any form of religious arrogance that says 'our truth is the only truth'. As I see ways to evoke heart and soul in preparing teachers for public schools, I want neither to violate the wall of separation between church and state, nor to encourage those who would violate the conventions of others. But I am equally passionate about not violating the deepest needs of the human soul, which education does with some regularity.
>
> *(p. 379)*

Yet, I do recognize embracing the support of spirituality would pose a second conundrum for teachers. If it can be done within constitutional parameters, then the question seems to be, how do we do it? And, for those preparing educators to teach, the question emerging seems to be, what do we need to provide them in order to do so?

Importance of a Holistic View of the Child and Inclusion of Spirituality in the Curriculum

In the U.S. the profession of early childhood education (ECE), encompassing the ages of birth to eight, is overseen by the National Association for the Education of Young Children (NAEYC), which accredits ECE teacher preparation programs housed in both private and public higher education institutions across the nation. NAEYC's guiding beacon is the advancement of Developmentally Appropriate Practices (DAP). DAP imply that teachers center their teaching around practices that understand child development and find their starting point for facilitating learning in the children's interests and needs. DAP is a big proponent of holistic education, in which the child is understood as a whole, integral person, comprising different areas of development, primarily: physical, cognitive, language, and socio-emotional development. DAP is also very much concerned with equity and inclusion in education and meeting the diverse needs of children from different cultural and linguistic backgrounds (Copple & Bredekamp, 2009). However, I believe NAEYC's DAP's understanding of the child as a whole is still missing the spiritual component even after recently revising their position statement and seminal text (NAEYC, 2022), to be more inclusive of diversity and the promotion of equity in all aspects of early childhood education including planning, teaching, assessing, and working with families and communities.

In the introduction to Part I of the *International Handbook of Holistic Education*, Novak (2019) explains he found seven integrated dimensions of holistic education: three related to our organic nature reflected as (1) **natural holism**, comprising the neurological dimension (our brains are hardwired for holism), the

How Can We Nurture Children's Spirituality in Secular Settings? **129**

incarnated dimension (we think through our bodies), and the aesthetic dimension of the person (our first education comes through the feeling perception of beautiful things in the world). Three related to the beginnings, middle, and prospective fulfillment of our being in the world presented as (2) **cultural holism**, including the anthropological dimension (before 'civilization' all human education was holistic), the historic dimension (diverse wisdom traditions provide manifold educative resources for the recovery of our natural wholeness within 'civilization'), and the philosophical dimension of being (bringing the left brain to know what the right brain can do). And lastly, a single overarching dimension named (3) **holism and the soul**, including the soulful dimension of humans (Psyche and Eros as the fundamental matter and method of human education).

NAEYC's DAP seems to embrace natural holism by advocating for concrete, hands-on, experiential ways of learning, and to some extent, it has begun to take into account cultural holism, by revising its developmentally based approaches to teaching through an inclusive and equity-based framework, to include diverse learners, both racially and linguistically, and within a spectrum of abilities. Yet, it does not seem to include holism and the soul, as the child's spirit or soul is not mentioned and does not seem to be part of the NAEYC discourse. In contrast, my approach to educating children stems from an understanding of the child as a whole human being, including body, mind, and soul, and thus aligns itself well with the soulful dimension of holism.

Later on, in the first chapter of the *International Handbook of Holistic Education* (Miller et al., 2019), John P. Miller (2019) shares a brief history of holistic education, beginning with when the term was first introduced in 1988 by Ron Miller and John P. Miller himself. He shares that Ron Miller (1988) explained holistic education as,

> an expression of profound respect for the deeper, largely unrealized powers of our human nature. Holistic educators see each child as a precious gift, as an embryo of untapped spiritual potential. This attitude is similar to the Quaker belief that there is 'that of God in every one' – or at least an unfathomed depth of personality, contained in the soul of every person.
>
> *(p. 2)*

Back in 1988, in the first edition of *The Holistic Curriculum*, John P. Miller (1988) presented holistic education as having its focus on relationships: "between linear thinking and intuition, . . . between mind and body, . . . between various domains of knowledge, . . . between the individual and community, and . . . between self and Self" (p. 3). In later editions (Miller, 1996, 2007), Miller also included the connection to the earth and replaced the use of the word 'Self' with the word 'soul', strengthening the connection between holistic education and spirituality.

130 Tying It All Together

It is with this understanding of holism, recognizing the divine in the child which presents itself through the child's soul, and focusing on building relationships and connections with self, with others, and with the Other, that I frame the work I do in preparing early childhood educators. Next, I share how I have begun preparing pre-service teachers for the art of nurturing children's spirituality, and the different ways in which it can be facilitated even in secular settings as found in the literature and research.

Nurturing Spirituality in the Classroom – The Role of the Teacher

In my role as a teacher educator, I have taught courses on child development, assessment, curriculum design, teaching methods, and second language acquisition, yet I had not taught a course dedicated to my line of research inquiry: children's spirituality. Thus, a few years ago, I decided to redesign a capstone internship seminar on early childhood education (ECE) I was teaching. I began by asking my students, pre-service teacher candidates, to read about children's spirituality, design a two-week meditation project to carry out with the children in their internship, practice different meditation techniques introduced to them weekly, and also engage in weekly lectures and discussions on topics related to children's spirituality. In reading the discussion boards in which my students express their thoughts on children's spirituality and how, in their role as teachers, they would support spirituality for both themselves and their colleagues, and the children under their charge, I discovered the depth these pre-service teachers were bringing to the field.

After completing the readings for the week, I asked my students what their main takeaways were regarding what children's spirituality means for the field of ECE, and for them as early childhood educators. This is what some of my students shared:

> After reading this book (Mata, 2015) I started to reconsider the way I view education and my role as a teacher. Throughout my learning experiences in the classroom, I have started to connect with the idea that a teacher's role is to make sure students are learning in everything they are doing. As teachers, I believe we have the ability to see everything as a learning opportunity, but as potential spiritual friends, we also have the opportunity to turn a learning experience into a spiritually uplifting opportunity. Our focus is on the whole child and while it can be easy to focus our attention solely on curriculum and education, we must remember that our students are more than growing brains; they are learners with souls that see the world around them in different ways and through unique lenses. Because of this, I believe it is necessary for teachers to incorporate opportunities for the students to express whom they are in the

spiritual world allowing others to see the whole them and not just the learners they sit next to in class. Whether it is through show and tell or an 'all about you' autobiography, I believe students should have the opportunity to spiritually express themselves in ECE.

(Thalia, 15 November 2020)

Another student-teacher candidate shared,

Overall, I think that children's spirituality means so much for early childhood education as a field, and for early childhood educators (teachers) in particular. This is because early childhood education focuses so heavily on all of the needs a child has, rather than just academics. In ECE, we are continuously planning and implementing lessons/instruction/experiences that nurture the whole child (physically, mentally, socially, and emotionally). Additionally, as teachers, spirituality gives us many opportunities to be in the moment, relax, meditate, and reflect, and so much more. This is extremely important as teaching ECE can be extremely overwhelming at times.

(Erika, 11 November 2020)

And lastly, another pre-service teacher shared her enthusiasm in realizing the role that spirituality can potentially have in classrooms,

Wow!!! This week's readings were everything!! There were so many great takeaways that I am excited to use and share in my teaching practice. First, let me start off by expressing, I love this quote "children are spiritual beings as much as they are rational, emotional, physical, and intellectual" (Mata, 2015, p. 120). After reading that quote, I realized just as much as I nurture and feed my students' emotional, physical, and intellectual skills. . . . I need to do the same with their spirituality. I can do this by creating an environment that nurtures students' pride. For example, I can ask students to bring an item into the classroom space. This item can be something that the student respects, values, confides in, or believes in. Giving the student the opportunity to share the connection they have with the object, allows them to open up about their spirituality. Likewise, I can create an environment where students feel free to express themselves through music, arts, and imaginative play. This will bring students a joyful experience and will encourage them to share their spirituality with other people. I can make it a priority of mine to be in touch with my spirituality, so students will feel encouraged to share such a joyous experience. There are so many different ways I can foster a spirituality-friendly atmosphere for my students, however, the best way I can nurture my student spirituality is by becoming 'The Soulful Teacher'. "If teaching is done from the

132 Tying It All Together

soul, teachers can see themselves in their students and their students in them. Teaching then becomes an act in which learning can occur in an atmosphere of freedom, love, and respect" (Mata, 2015, p. 130). The more students feel the freedom to express their individuality, the more awakened their spirituality becomes.

(Katie, 14 November 2020)

These teacher candidates expressed their understanding of spirituality as a means to support the whole child. They made evident that by nurturing the child's spirit they see a possibility to support their development beyond the cognitive, literacy, and linguistic skills typically comprising the focus of the curriculum. After reading and discussing the topic of spirituality as one that could be facilitated in education, they began to understand their roles as more than a facilitator of skills, content, and knowledge, and they shared their comprehension that in their role lies a wealth of possibility in mediating learning for children through every experience, especially those in which the child shares their spirit and essence. These pre-service teachers also realized that, by embracing spirituality in the classroom, they were opening spaces for themselves to be supported spiritually as well and appreciated being able to take the time to pause, engage in mediation, and be more present in their daily tasks.

In answering a different discussion board prompt, when asked which activities presented in the readings would they implement with their students and why my students shared the following:

One strategy I can use to support spirituality for the students at my internship site is the practice of giving children the freedom to have their own feelings, thoughts, and imagination. This strategy stood out to me the most because very often children are told to not feel a certain way, or to stop crying, etc. Especially in our virtual setting this semester, many children are going through a lot and may be dealing with emotions that they might have never dealt with before. So, it is important that we as educators take the time to have children share and be there for them as support and a listening ear. This has been something that I have been extremely mindful about because everyone's thoughts/feelings/emotions are valid and should be valued. So, all in all, I think it is so important to remind students that nothing is ever too small or too big to share.

(Erika, 11 November 2020)

A teacher can nurture spirituality through positive affirmations (reassuring the child's worth), asking children their thoughts/ideas (really talking to them), and "pushing" them (knowing that the child can do more/is capable of more-whether that is being kind or getting their work done). One way that I can

How Can We Nurture Children's Spirituality in Secular Settings?   **133**

help to support spirituality for the children in my internship site is "Waking Up." Waking up is being present and mindful. I think being fully present and mindful in my placement is important for me and my students, especially since we are not in a traditional classroom setting. It can be hard at times for both myself and the students to be fully present, as being in our homes for school can bring obstacles and distractions

(Sarah, 11 November 2020)

In thinking about how spirituality could be supported in the classroom and what could be done to incorporate spiritual nourishment for their students, these pre-service teachers realized the power listening to children had for their overall development, as well as providing them with the freedom and encouraging them to be fully present in order to express their authentic selves.

Through focusing on children's spirituality and completing the different activities and assignments in this redesigned seminar, my students began to open their understanding to the importance of nurturing the whole child, including the spirit. Laura summarized the experience beautifully,

So how do we do this in a salient way in the classroom? We model expressions of wonder and awe when we are learning. We teach children to be curious and reinforce their engagement by offering extensions to deeper learning about the things they are passionate about. We teach children to allow themselves to be inspired. We do this by creating space and capacity through meditation, breathing exercises, and a mindful openness to the present moment. In general, we know that our sense of wonder tends to dissipate as we age if left unattended. I think this occurs largely because we are distracted by the busyness we've constructed in our daily lives, but I think it's also due to a lack of understanding about the importance of spirituality. As teachers, we have a responsibility to nurture this innate sense of awe and curiosity, which I suppose can be labeled spirituality. Or maybe it doesn't require a label but simply an understanding of its importance in personal growth and enlightenment. As teachers, we have a responsibility to value each individual child and accept them for who they are, and it's this spiritual experience that connects us all. It is the human condition to desire connections with one another. We just need to awaken the spirit that's right there within us and in our students.

(Laura, 10 November 2020)

After participating in the seminar, my pre-service student teachers completed a post-survey as part of a research study I was conducting on the redesign of this seminar (in preparation) and seem to have embraced the notion of nourishing spirituality in the secular classroom, given the importance they realize it has for children's learning and development and that they, in their role as a teacher, can

134 Tying It All Together

and should facilitate spiritual support and nourishment for children, particularly if embracing a holistic notion of the child.

Nevertheless, this does not seem to be the case in other countries, even those that have compulsory religious education as part of their national curricula. Anita Gracie and Jacqueline Wilkinson (2022) conducted a study with 199 student teachers, between the ages of 17 and 22 years, in two different education systems – Northern Ireland and the Republic of Ireland, to determine why some students were reluctant to include spiritual activities as part of their teaching methods in the Religious Education (RE) classroom and to assess whether experiences of and training in these activities as part of their initial teacher education degrees would result in a measurable change of their attitudes, propelling them to attempt such activities in the future.

Through an online survey administered to 199 pre-service teachers, Gracie and Wilkinson (2022) set to determine which factors in a student teacher's identity made it more or less likely that they would incorporate spiritual activities in their classroom. Following, a series of workshops on spirituality was organized in each institution for a small group of approximately 30 students, on selected spirituality-based activities and presentations delivered by experts. Some of the students who attended the workshops also participated in focus group interviews.

When it came to 'active' exercises, researchers found that writing prayers were the most highly scored activity by pre-service teachers, only surpassed by stillness activities like listening to peaceful music and watching the calm jar settle. Activities that students were not prepared to try in their classrooms were a silent reflection on a religious image/symbol and meditation on a concept. The reasons why they would not engage in these activities

> ranged from not having enough knowledge or understanding of themselves (personal identity) to not wanting to indoctrinate or force a belief activity on children (teacher role), not being certain activities were consonant with the school ethos (teacher role) to not being confident in conducting the activities appropriately and so as not to cause offense.
>
> *(training/resources) (p. 10)*

Regarding religious identities, Gracie and Wilkinson (2022) found a clear link between a student teacher's religious identity and the type of spiritual activity they were willing to try in the classroom. Roman Catholic students were significantly more likely to attempt the suggested activities than those of other religious identities. Students who identified no religion showed the greatest range of answers and were more willing to try activities that seemed to be less faith-based.

From the focus groups and interviews, issues mentioned by students regarding facilitating spiritual activities in the classroom showed confidence regarding their own knowledge or skills as the issue with the highest frequency, and classroom

How Can We Nurture Children's Spirituality in Secular Settings? **135**

practice and behavior management as the second highest, with own faith and religious beliefs as the third. When asked what will encourage them to facilitate more of these activities in the classroom, 89% of all students indicated that they would like more training and more resources provided to be better prepared and more confident in their delivery of spiritual activities in the primary classroom.

In a study I conducted while I was in graduate school (Mata, 2012), through interviews of six in-service early childhood teachers and colleagues of mine,[1] I set to uncover if in-service teachers believed spirituality had a place in the secular classroom and if so, how would they facilitate it for their young students. Findings showed teachers did believe spirituality should be supported in the classroom, yet not necessarily through the curriculum and instructional content, yet more so through intentionally planned routines throughout the daily school schedule, such as reading an inspirational poem at the start of the day or engaging in conversation when children spontaneously posed big existential questions. One teacher offered,

> Within the classroom we are looking at children to ponder those still unanswered questions, those deep thoughts that really linger and raise right or wrong answers . . . we work on getting them to really ponder those unanswered questions, getting them to have those dialogues and make them consider alternate views of thinking about the world, your place in the world, your role in the world and all those interconnected relationships.
>
> *(Mata, 2012, p. 242)*

Other ways offered by the in-service teachers I interviewed were to plan for activities that promote community building such as encouraging sharing, empathy, and niceness in the classroom. Others spoke of offering opportunities to connect spiritually through music, children's literature, and open-ended, child-initiated play. Similar to Gracie and Wilkinson's (2022) students, these teachers also mentioned not having any prior training on children's spiritual development or how to promote it in the classroom.

Even though Gracie and Wilkinson's (2022) study was conducted in countries with compulsory religious education curricula, and a high population of pre-service teachers who are religious in faith and practice, it is interesting that in order for their pre-service teachers to feel confident in supporting children's spirituality, confidence in knowledge and skills to facilitate this in classrooms seems to be a prerequisite and was even requested. This is similar to my findings with in-service teachers teaching in secular settings in the U.S., who also thought they would widely benefit from training in how to support and nourish spirituality for children (Mata, 2012). It seems that be it for religious-based or secular education, there seems to be a need for teacher education programs to better embrace spirituality in their teacher preparation courses if the soul is to be included in the

136 Tying It All Together

nourishment provided to the whole child in schools. How to do this in higher education will be further explored in Chapter 7.

What Are Teachers Doing in the Classroom From a Secular Spirituality Perspective?

Given DAP does not include the spiritual component of development within their guidelines for practice with young children, we could easily assume that early childhood educators in the U.S. are not supporting children's spirituality. Yet, this does not seem to be the case. Since 2016, I have been leading a survey-based research study, working closely with two colleagues in the field of early childhood education, with the goal to gauge what early childhood educators in the U.S. are doing in order to support and nurture spirituality for children, ages zero to eight, in secular educational settings.

Based on the existing literature on children's spirituality, we designed a five-section survey, focusing on (1) spiritual views and practices, (2) activities and curriculum, (3) classroom environment and schedule, (4) interactions and experiences in school and community, and (5) demographic information. The survey has a total of 36 rating scale items, five open-ended questions, and 12 multiple-choice demographic questions.

Our guiding research questions were, (RQ1) How do in-service early childhood educators understand children's spirituality? (RQ2) Do in-service early childhood educators, working with children ages birth to eight, perceive themselves as intentionally nurturing and supporting spirituality in their secular classrooms? And if so, (RQ3) What specific experiences, activities, and/or strategies are being used in the classroom, and the school as a whole, to support children's spirituality? (Mata-McMahon et al., 2020).

We distributed the survey online, sending it directly to early childhood educators via email and also distributing it at early childhood education conferences. We collected 33 responses from educators. Our respondents had the following characteristics: 31 females, two males; 24 white and nine Hispanic/Latino; 14 general education teachers, six specialists, two special education teachers, and 11 identifying as other. Regarding years of experience, 25 had 10 or more years of experience, five had 3–5 years of experience, two had 6–9 years of experience, and one had 1–2 years of experience. Respondents worked primarily with pre-schoolers (n = 22), while four worked with toddlers, three with third graders, two with kindergarteners, and two with first graders. More educators worked in private (n = 22) than public (n = 12) secular schools. All respondents were working with children in the U.S., representing 16 different states. Respondents came from urban settings (n = 17), suburban settings (n = 12), and rural settings (n = 4) (Mata-McMahon et al., 2018).

In two separate papers, we shared the results found through the five open-ended survey questions and answered our three research questions. For RQ1, we found that most of the early childhood educators surveyed have a multilayered understanding of children's spirituality and most commonly believe that it includes building connections, practicing virtues, and making meaning of the world. The surveyed educators placed more emphasis on inter-personal character traits related to the heart, and to a lesser degree mentioned God and religion, self-awareness, mindfulness and presence, humanness, and inner feelings as part of their understanding of spirituality (Mata-McMahon et al., 2020). These results are further explained in Chapter 3.

Regarding RQ2, our findings suggested that most early childhood educators surveyed do indeed perceive themselves as intentionally nurturing and supporting spirituality in their secular classrooms. In answering RQ3, we found that early childhood educators reported nurturing children's spirituality by providing opportunities for creative expression and free play, engagement with nature, contemplative practices (e.g., mindfulness), relationship building, and moral/character development activities. As mentions of creative expressions, the following were the most salient,

> *Music* played a significant role in nurturing children's spirituality, supporting relaxation and concentration. *Storytelling* was used to communicate the worthiness of children's worldviews, as well as to stimulate the imagination. One participant described sharing books with children to "promote open-ended perspectives (such as books about death or fill a bucket)" (code 2.1.2). Another stated that "discussions of motivation and values of characters" (code 2.1.2) are used while reading stories along with "questions to stimulate consideration of principles" (code 2.1.2). *Art* was described as an integral part of classroom instruction including painting, finger painting, and drawing. Respondents also described using "collaborative artwork and project work" (code 2.1.3) and discussing the art of others. *Body movement* included dancing and stretching. One educator shared that dance activities help children to appreciate the simple joy of being present.
>
> *(Mata-McMahon et al., 2018, p. 2244)*

It was encouraging to find that early childhood educators in the U.S. are finding such varied ways to support children's spirituality in their secular educational settings in ways that overlap with the developmentally appropriate practices they already provide *(Mata-McMahon et al., 2018)*.[2]

In another study I conducted with pre-service teachers enrolled in an early childhood education teacher preparation program, I worked with 11 teacher candidates who participated in an online discussion forum after a three-hour workshop session on the topic of children's spirituality (Mata, 2014). The participating

138 Tying It All Together

pre-service teachers were all female, with ages ranging between 20 and 50 years, and their racial backgrounds were: Hispanic (n=5), White (n=3), and Black (n=3). Three of the participants had been born abroad and English was their second language. The teacher candidates were asked to participate in the online discussion forum by (1) sharing their thoughts on spirituality, how they understood it, how they defined it, and what it meant to them, and (2) explaining if they thought spirituality had a place in early childhood education, and if so, providing examples of how they would incorporate it in their classroom with their own students.

Regarding how they would support spirituality in their classroom, there seemed to be two major lines of action. Some teacher candidates related supporting spirituality with incorporating nature into the classroom and facilitating children's appreciation of nature. Others spoke of facilitating a state of mind as spiritual support, by helping children to calm their minds in order to better reflect and ponder the world around them.

Regarding mentions of contact with nature, one participant shared:

> we may not realize it but we do bring our spirituality into the classroom when we bring in leaves, twigs, [when we] plant flowers, grow gardens, explore how things came to be. [These] are all spirituality, and we incorporate it without calling it spirituality.

(p. 117)

Another shared, "I think incorporating nature into the everyday curriculum can help students feel more connected [to] the world around them. . . . Appreciation for nature is so often lost in the later grades, which makes it even more important that we cover it in early childhood" (p. 118).

Regarding promoting a calm state of mind, a pre-service teacher mentioned, "I do believe spirituality can be achieved in the classroom through a brief daily moment of silence/reflection. By giving special attention to one's own self, breathing pattern, and/or thoughts, children can subconsciously connect with their inner being" (p. 118). And another shared, "I think meditation and yoga [are] the best ways to include spirituality. It gives children the time to relax and soothe themselves. [Through yoga and meditation] one must become in-tune with self to appreciate and value who he or she is" (118).

In a piece that initially seems to be making a case for how early childhood teachers can support spiritual development by encouraging pre-schoolers to share their dreams and inner thoughts, Kathleen Harris (2013) explains how project-based learning has all the components consistent with developmentally appropriate practices to help teachers nurture spirituality in the classroom, while also meeting children's needs and interests by being a research effort deliberately focused on finding solutions to questions about a topic posed by the children, the teachers, or the teacher working with the children (Helm & Katz, 2001). Harris explains how

How Can We Nurture Children's Spirituality in Secular Settings? **139**

through an eight-week project-based unit, entitled the dream project, teachers were able to design curricular activities stemming from children's shared dreams and promote creative thinking by integrating children's culture boosting balance, integrity, and reciprocal relationships, and strengthening the community within the classroom and the school at large. The project-based unit encouraged children to ask inquiring questions, make predictions and hypothesize, promote creativity, and practice multimodal ways of thinking and representing thinking in graphic, written, and oral language.

A study conducted in New Zealand with 24 teachers working with the early childhood curriculum *Te Whāriki* (Greenfield, 2018) looked into how teachers understood and facilitated spirituality or *wairua* in the classroom.[3] Even though this curriculum is designed to support children spiritually, teachers still find it difficult to do this intentionally. Teachers shared they agree that teachers have a responsibility to care for, protect, and respect each child. Teachers explained that in order to do this they use prayer, promote respectful relationships, provide an environment where children can express themselves freely and talk about what is important to them, listen to children and their families, promote kindness, foster secure attachments, facilitate connections to nature, model behaviors they want children to emulate, provide opportunities for children to care for others, celebrate different cultures and religious festivals, give hugs, see beyond the external behavior, and are genuinely interested in the children they care for.

In summary, early childhood educators across different countries and especially in the U.S. seem to agree on the importance of nurturing children's spirituality and view their role as fundamental in providing this support in the classroom. The ways in which teachers provide this support vary, yet they seem to agree that even if there is a curriculum in place that includes spiritual development, it is up to the teacher to find strategies and open spaces and time during the school day to honor the child's spirit as it is shared with them from the child. Child-initiated conversations, ponderings, and even units of study seem to be the developmentally appropriate ways in which teachers can make sure spirituality is honored, having the child take the lead and initiate the conversation seems to be the most common approach to ensure spiritual nurturing.

Notes

1. This study is first introduced and explained in Chapter 3. There the focus is on in-service teachers understanding of spirituality. In this chapter the focus is on these teachers' perceptions of spirituality belonging in the classroom and how they would facilitate this nourishment.
2. This project is ongoing. We currently are in the process of publishing the validation study of this survey Mata-McMahon et al. (under review), as an instrument entitled *Early Childhood Educators' Spiritual Practices in the Classroom (ECE-SPC)*, to collect further data from a larger sample of early childhood educators across the U.S. and potentially abroad, once the instrument is adapted and translated to reflect other cultures and

140 Tying It All Together

languages. Furthermore, we plan to convert the survey into a rating scale, teachers can use on their own to self-assess their efforts to support and nurture children's spirituality through their curriculum, classroom environment, and overall school community.

3. This study is presented in more detail in Chapter 3.

References

Carpenter, W. A. (2003). Jacob's children and ours: Richard of St. Victor's curriculum of the soul. *Educational Horizons, 82*(1), 44–54.

Copple, C., & Bredekamp, S. (Eds.). (2009). *Developmentally appropriate practice in early childhood programs: Serving children from birth to age 8* (3rd ed.). NAEYC.

Freire, P. (1997). *Pedagogy of the oppressed* (M. Bergman Ramos, Trans., New Revised 20th Anniversary ed.). Continuum.

Gracie, A., & Wilkinson, J. (2022). Mindfulness, meditation and me: Student Teachers' willingness to engage with spiritual activities in the primary school classroom. *International Journal of Children's Spirituality, 27*(1), 1–19. https://doi.org/10.1080/13644 36X.2022.2101988

Greenfield, C. F. (2018). Investigation into New Zealand early childhood teachers' perspectives on spirituality and Wairua in teaching. *International Journal of Children's Spirituality, 23*(3), 275–290. https://doi.org/10.1080/1364436X.2018.1460333

Harris, K. (2013). Teacher, I had a dream: A glimpse of the spiritual domain of children using project-based learning. *International Journal of Children's Spirituality, 18*(3), 281–293. https://doi.org/10.1080/1364436X.2013.858665

Helm, J. H., & Katz, L. G. (2001). *Young investigators: The project approach in the early years.* Teachers College Press.

Mata, J. (2012). Nurturing spirituality in early childhood classrooms: The teacher's view. In M. Fowler, J. D. Martin, & J. L. Hochheimer (Eds.), *Spirituality: Theory, praxis and pedagogy* (pp. 239–248). Inter-Disciplinary Press.

Mata, J. (2014). Sharing my journey and opening spaces: Spirituality in the classroom. *International Journal of Children's Spirituality, 19*(2), 112–122. https://doi.org/10.1080/1364436X.2014.922464

Mata, J. (2015). *Spiritual experiences in early childhood education: Four kindergarteners, one classroom.* Routledge.

Mata-McMahon, J., Haslip, M. J., & Kruse, L. (under review). Validation study of the Early Childhood Educators' Spiritual Practices in the Classroom (ECE-SPC) instrument using rasch. *International Journal of Children's Spirituality.*

Mata-McMahon, J., Haslip, M. J., & Schein, D. L. (2018). Early childhood educators' perceptions of nurturing spirituality in secular settings. *Early Child Development and Care, 189*(14), 2233–2251. https://doi.org/10.1080/03004430.2018.1445734

Mata-McMahon, J., Haslip, M. J., & Schein, D. L. (2020). Connections, virtues, and meaning-making: How early childhood educators describe children's spirituality. *Early Childhood Education Journal, 48*(5), 657–669. https://doi.org/10.1007/s10643-020-01026-8

Miller, J. P. (1988). *The Holistic curriculum.* OISE Press.

Miller, J. P. (1996). *The Holistic curriculum* (2nd ed.). OISE Press.

Miller, J. P. (2007). *The Holistic curriculum* (3rd ed.). OISE Press.

Miller, J. P. (2019). Holistic education: A brief history. In J. P. Miller, K. Nigh, J. B. Marni, B. Novak, & S. Crowell (Eds.), *International handbook of Holistic education* (pp. 5–16). Routledge.

Miller, J. P., Nigh, K., Binder, M. J., Novak, B., & Crowell, S. (Eds.). (2019). *International handbook of Holistic education*. Routledge.

Miller, R. (1988). Holistic education: A radical perspective. *The Holistic Education Review*, *1*(1), 2–3.

Montessori, M. (1912). *The Montessori method* (A. E. George, Trans.). Frederick A. Stokes Company.

NAEYC. (2022). *Developmentally appropriate practice in early childhood programs serving children from birth through age 8* (4th ed.). National Association for the Education of Young Children (NAEYC).

National Archives (2018). *The bill of rights: A transcription*. National Archives and Records Administration. Retrieved September 11, 2022, from www.archives.gov/founding-docs/bill-of-rights-transcript

National History Education Clearinghouse (2018). *Separation of church and state*. Retrieved September 11, 2022, from https://teachinghistory.org/history-content/ask-a-historian/24441 (© 2018 Created by the Roy Rosenzweig Center for History and New Media at George Mason University with funding from the U.S. Department of Education (Contract Number ED-07-CO-0088))

Novak, B. (2019). Part I foundations – introduction. In J. P. Miller, K. Nigh, M. J. Binder, B. Novak, & S. Crowell (Eds.), *International handbook of Holistic Education* (pp. 1–4). Routledge.

Palmer, P. J. (1993). *To know as we are known: Education as a spiritual journey*. Harper.

Palmer, P. J. (2003). Teaching with heart and soul: Reflections on spirituality in teacher education. *Journal of Teacher Education*, *54*(5), 376–385. https://doi.org/10.1177/0022487103257359

Sanderson, N. (2022, September 15). *On spirituality*. Electronic communication.

Snyder, J. R. (2014). *Tending the light: Essays on Montessori education*. North American Montessori Teachers' Association.

7

SPIRITUALITY AS THE NORTH STAR FOR EARLY CHILDHOOD EDUCATION

Where Do We Go From Here?

In a recent email communication from the Vice-President of the American Educational Research Association's (AERA's) Teaching & Teacher Education – Division K, Marianna Souto-Manning pledges to continue the much-needed work and movement toward a more just future. She states,

> Our field is at a crossroads. COVID-19 made it impossible to ignore inequities and harms in schooling, yet the discourse has quickly shifted from reimagining schooling to repairing and remediating what has been called the "learning loss." These reparative narratives of crises and racial capitalistic paradigms pathologically shape teaching and teacher education. It is in times like this when we don't know what to do or how to deal with our anger, fear, and the sense of uncertainty, that the field can benefit from being guided by what Savannah Shange called "a North Star logic" in the book *Progressive Dystopia: Abolition, Antiblackness, and Schooling in San Francisco* (2019).
> *(Souto-Manning, 2022) (email communication, September 8, 2022, para. 1)*

Shange (2019) explains that a North Star logic is predicated on designing, envisioning, and bringing to life futures that are very different from the past. Souto-Manning explains that as a field, we need to reject tendencies to continue to do what is expected and respected as established research agendas, policies, and practices in teaching and teacher education. She makes a call for us, collectively, needing to focus on the potentiality of teaching and teacher education, without the naivete of focusing on this potential without considering the obstacles that our societal systemic trauma and oppression represent. She foreshadows that there has been, and there will continue to be, the kind of resistance

DOI: 10.4324/9781003081463-10

Spirituality as the North Star for Early Childhood Education **143**

and "friction produced in the encounter between racialized futures and pasts" (Shange, 2019, p. 65).

Souto-Manning (2022) is clearly speaking of inequities in education based on systemic racial issues that have plagued the U.S. historically and asserts that the days of teaching and teacher education research, policies, and practices centered on whiteness are far from gone. She explains that we can no longer ignore the harm teaching and teacher education have inflicted in perpetuating our systems of oppression and forewarns that to address and repair this harm we must enact robust commitment toward racial justice and social transformation within our educational system. I agree with her call to action and would venture to add that this call should not be limited to promoting repairs pertaining to the social and racial injustices we currently live through, yet include the whole human being, and consider that these injustices involve much more than just the color of our skin, affecting who we are as whole humans, including the effects they have on our soul.

Supporting Children's Spirituality Starting in Higher Education

As Shange and Souto-Manning explain, education has the potential to become the guiding North Star for society, particularly after the conditions society has endured during COVID-19 (e.g., job loss, social isolation, and lockdowns leading to an increase in domestic violence, and death), allowing for a shift in paradigm that could start with an overhaul of how we teach and prepare teachers to teach. I propose, including secular spirituality, as explained in Chapter 1, in education. Understanding the spiritual as an intrinsic and fundamental component of who we are as human beings can propel us forward into the change we are overdue for as a society, prompting a world in which we value soul and spirit over material wealth. As a teacher educator, it is from this vantage point, that I propose the change to begin. Through teacher preparation programs, we can begin to boost the transformation toward a spiritually inclusive education system, without having to wait for much-needed legislative and policy changes (e.g., requiring the spiritual domain to be facilitated through early childhood curricula) that may take decades to be enacted.

In a study I conducted observing kindergarteners in their secular classrooms (Mata, 2015), I found common threads in how children experience and express spirituality. Specifically, I found that "(a) joy, its expression, and its enjoyment; (b) concern for others through a display of kindness, compassion, and care; (c) the importance of relationships and the value given to friends and family; and (d) the use and exploration of imagination" (p. 103) were the salient ways in which the kindergarteners I observed experienced and express themselves spiritually.

I found that a spiritual experience for kindergarteners was "any experience through which the child can express their joy, their compassion, and kindness, their sense of relating to others, or their creative and imaginative self" (Mata, 2015, p. 117). Additionally, these experiences could be outwardly or inwardly

144 Tying It All Together

triggered and sometimes could "provoke pondering and searching through inner thought and conversations" (Mata, 2015, p. 117), although mainly, they manifested themselves ordinarily in everyday activity.

With this understanding of how spirituality can be experienced and expressed by children in secular educational environments, I set to make an impact in the preparation of pre-service teachers who will be teaching young children. In my teacher preparation courses, I urge teachers to prepare themselves in addressing and allowing for children's spiritual expressions and experiences to occur in their classrooms. Because the focus is on secularity, I encourage them to approach nurturing spirituality with the understanding of the differentiation between the concepts of religion and spirituality in order for these spiritual expressions and experiences to be nurtured and supported in public, secular settings. With this understanding, teachers can support the whole child, including the body, mind, and soul through their pedagogies and instructional strategies, by providing the time and space for children to experience and express themselves spiritually as they learn and develop while in school.

The question that often arises when this proposition is offered, by those who embrace fostering the child's spirit is, "yes, but how do we do this?" How do we best prepare educators to support children holistically, including the spirit and the soul? In the next section of this chapter, I present a few initiatives for teachers that have been successful in preparing them for this most important part of their role as educators.

What Do We Need to Do? Where Do We Start?

In compiling empirical works for this book, I came across several studies conducted with early childhood educators in which the researchers were looking into how spirituality was being supported in the classroom. Either through a given, mandated curriculum or through pedagogical initiatives designed by teachers, they try their best to follow the regulations of their country's department of education to support children's spiritual development.

In many cases, teachers report not having sufficient support or training, and not being adequately prepared to nurture children's spirituality; neither do they have any level of certainty that what they are doing, even when following curricular guidelines, indeed contributes to their student's spiritual growth (Farrell et al., 2020; Greenfield, 2018; Mata, 2012, 2013a, 2013b; Robinson, 2019; Vuorinen et al., 2021).

Very few initiatives, if any, have been designed with the goal of preparing teachers to explore their spiritual selves or inviting them to nurture and support their students' spirits. Parker Palmer's Courage to Teach, presented later, is one program that has been quite successful in the U.S. in the past decades (Center for Courage & Renewal, 2022).

In teaching with Heart and Soul, Parker Palmer (2003), an educator from the U.S. who has more than three decades of exploring, writing about, and working with educators on the spiritual dimensions of K-12 and higher education,

Spirituality as the North Star for Early Childhood Education **145**

explores two very important questions: Is there a 'spiritual' dimension to good teaching? And, if so, do spiritual considerations have a place in teacher education? Palmer believes the answer to both these questions is affirmative.

Palmer (2003) explains that teachers should not limit themselves to their role of teaching a specific subject matter, but should never stop asking of their students: "who is this child, and how can I nurture his or her gifts?" (p. 377). These questions connect teachers to their students in ways that make evident the depth of their vocation: to teach not mathematics but the child, and to provide the educational experience with a spiritual element that otherwise is missing from teaching. He explains the definition of spirituality he has found most useful and simple is, "spirituality is the eternal yearning to be connected with something larger than our own egos" (p. 377).

Over years of scholarship, Palmer (2003) has developed a 'pedagogy of the soul' taught through the Courage to Teach (CTT) program for K-12 educators across the country.

> The typical CTT group consists of 25 K-12 educators, from a variety of schools in a region, who take a 2-year journey through eight-weekend retreats, under the guidance of a trained facilitator. The purpose of these groups can be stated simply: to provide public school education with a space where it is safe for their souls to show up and make a claim on the work they do.
>
> (p. 380)

The CTT program has made inroads into public education as well as migrated across professional lines, particularly into the medical field, as medical certifying associations have realized that if a physician cannot connect with the 'heart and soul' of the patient, they are less likely to be healers than those who can.[1]

The link between soul and role has become critical in medicine, surely the same is true in education, where the relation of teacher and student must be deeply and wholly human for learning to occur. The question that arises is how do we address spiritual topics in public education that respect the vast diversity of people's deeply held traditions and beliefs?

In the CTT program for educators, the question is answered by framing the two-year journey with metaphors from the seasons. Palmer (2003) explains, "hosted by the seasonal metaphors, we are encouraged to speak about issues we often evade – and to do so in the language most meaningful to whoever is speaking – without anyone giving or taking offense" (p. 380). For example, in the fall season, when nature plants her seeds, the CTT group inquires into "the seed of true self," taking participants into autobiographical reflection, sharing childhood stories revealing something of whom they were before social deformations set in.

Then moving into winter, participants come to understand that whatever was planted is now frozen, buried deep, dead, or perhaps dormant. Teachers share that when they begin to see what is dormant in themselves, they are better able to see what is dormant in their students and become better teachers in the process.

146 Tying It All Together

Spring is the season of surprises, where participants realize that the death that occurred in winter can give way to new life; for spring the metaphor used is "the flowering paradox," which Palmer (2003) explains,

> as winter's darkness and death give rise to their apparent opposites, spring invites us to contemplate the many both-ands we must hold to live life fully and well: The deeper our faith, the more doubt we must endure; the deeper our hope, the more prone we are to despair; the deeper our love, the more grief we are likely to know.

(p. 381)

As teachers understand spring's paradoxes, they gain insight into professional as well as personal growth, as they embrace many paradoxes in their daily work.

Finally, summer represents the season of abundance and harvest. Participants traced the seed of true self from birth, through dormancy, into flowering, now look at the abundance that has grown up within them and begin to ask, "Whom is it meant to feed?" "Where am I called to use my gifts in the world?" In the summer season, participants go beyond learning *who* they are to understand more about *whose* they are.

Over decades, the CTT groups, which hold divergent convictions, have been able to use the metaphors of the seasons to host powerful dialogues about critical questions and meaning. Palmer explains this is possible because, beneath our deep differences in belief and/or disbelief, we all share something much deeper: love embedded in the natural world and cycles of human experiences that echo the cycles of nature. He explains that the seasonal metaphors evoke our shared condition, providing a common ground where we can explore meaningful matters and experience connectedness. This connectedness then allows for teachers to replicate it in the classroom with their students.

This program is not without a set of rules and principles that participants and facilitators need to adhere to for it to be successful. Palmer explains that central to the pedagogy of the CTT is creating a space that welcomes the soul. This means that everything that is done within the groups is premised on certain assumptions about the soul's nature and needs, and about what will make the soul feel welcome.

These assumptions are rooted in another metaphor from nature: the soul is like a wild animal, and just like a wild animal the soul is tough, resilient, savvy, resourceful, self-sufficient, and knows what it needs to survive in hard places. Based on this premise, CTT depends on four main pedagogical principles and practices:

1. CTT groups are voluntary, and everything that happens within them is by invitation rather than command;
2. A simple ground rule is enforced over all the eight three-day retreats over two years regarding how to speak to each other: No fixing, no saving, no advising, no setting straight;

Spirituality as the North Star for Early Childhood Education **147**

3. We respond to each other by asking honest, open questions whose sole intent is to help hear each other into speech, deeper and deeper speech; and
4. The CTT program makes use of third things – poems, teaching stories, music, or works of art – that represent a voice other than that of the facilitator or a member of the group.

(Palmer, 2007)

The facilitator is also required to include personal qualities and professional skills making them capable of safeguarding a space where the soul feels welcome to show up.

The CTT has been evaluated thoroughly, via both qualitative and quantitative methods of analysis.[2] Yet all evaluations seem to converge and agree on the same results: "if you educate teachers' hearts and souls, they deepen their relations with students, restore community with colleagues, embrace new leadership roles on behalf of authentic educational reform, and renew their sense of vocation instead of dropping out" (Palmer, 2003, p. 384).

Even with the differences and constraints within higher education, I believe programs like the CTT can be replicated, or at least aspects of it can be facilitated in traditional teacher preparation programs. I believe in order to begin these conversations for pre-service teachers it is imperative that we start by inviting them to reflect on what spirituality means to each of us, both students and instructors. In order to provide spaces in which children can feel safe enough to share their ponderings and big questions, teachers first need to know what type of reflective space they are willing to provide, given how they understand and relate to spirituality themselves.

Recently, I redesigned the early childhood education (ECE) seminar I teach to teacher candidates completing their student teaching experience, to focus on the topic of spirituality and how to nurture it for children, through experiences of meditation in order to promote mindfulness in the classroom. In this seminar, I begin by asking my students, and teacher candidates, what spirituality means to them. I would suggest early childhood educators interested in promoting children's spirituality begin here, asking themselves, "How do I define and understand spirituality? If I had to explain spirituality to others, what would I say?" This is an important and introspective task as some of us define spirituality framed by the religious upbringing we might have had growing up.[3]

I invite my teacher-candidate students to engage in the exercise of reexamining their roots related to spirituality and finding their definition, whatever that might be, as the starting point, before even thinking of supporting or nurturing the spirituality of the children under their care. We typically do this not through a written, intellectual path, but I invite my students to use the medium of art to express what spirituality means for them.[4] Within this exercise, I also share my definition of spirituality and make a point of differentiating it from religiosity. I present spirituality as inclusive and linked to any given individual's beliefs, values, identities, ethical principles, mental health, or overall well-being. It can, of course,

148 Tying It All Together

be experienced through organized religion, yet need not be, and it can include the spiritual experiences of atheists and agnostics as well (Waggoner, 2016).

After we are clear in our understanding of what spirituality means to us, we can begin to engage in the business of thinking about how we will go about providing spaces and time within our daily classroom schedule and curricula, to nurture the spirit of the child and support their spiritual growth. To accomplish this, I present my students with the task of completing a meditation project with the children in their student teaching internship site. They are asked to select a learning objective they want their students to achieve. This can be a math or language arts objective, but typically my students select a behavioral objective, such as, "Students will be calmer and focused on the lesson, requiring less behavior reminders while learning after the meditation experience." After identifying the objective, they are asked to design a two-week meditation intervention presenting the children with 1- to 5-minute meditation experiences daily, for a span of two weeks. The duration of the meditation experiences will depend upon the age of the children, less time for younger children, and increased time for children in the higher grade levels. They are also asked to document the reactions of the children following the meditation technique they implement, and again document it at the end of the school day. Each week they are asked to reflect on the children's behavior and provide a summary as well as determine if and to what degree was the learning objective met.

This meditation project includes both conceptual, theoretical, and empirical-based readings, as well as practical applications and strategies to support children's spirituality. I also provide weekly 10-minute meditation techniques for them to practice and ask them to journal about their experience in order to help them reflect on the impact that practicing meditation might have on their teaching. These meditations and other resources, including a list of children's books, music tracks, and applications, which will help early childhood educators support spirituality in the classroom, can be found in my professional website.[5]

Thus far, I have taught two iterations of this redesigned ECE seminar course. In 2019, I taught eight undergraduate and graduate students; and most recently in 2020, I taught nine undergraduate and graduate early childhood teacher candidates. These students have been all female, come from different socio-economic backgrounds, and identify as African American, Latinx, White, Asian American, and Middle Eastern. Their ages ranged from 20 to 42 years. These are some of the reflections my students shared on the impact the weekly meditation had on their mindfulness experiences, and how in turn mindfulness affected their teaching and the ways they interacted with their students:

> The meditation techniques we have been engaging in along with the study of mindfulness has been personally helpful to me. I do find myself more mindful than I normally do during this time in the semester. The beautiful thing about mindfulness is that it is much like knowledge and truth one cannot truly engage with these things without some kind of change. Just the act of thinking about

Spirituality as the North Star for Early Childhood Education   **149**

mindfulness makes me more mindful. I realize that mindfulness looks a bit different for me then one may think. I tend to use the weekly meditations during my bedtime when I am trying to let go of the things of the day. Even though the meditation is at night I use techniques like deep breathing to center myself with students. This was mentioned in the Knowles reading for this week the need to establish personal mindfulness before asking it of our students. I think that it is one of the largest ideas I have learned thus far. This idea gives me even more cause to truly take care of myself so that I can take care of my students.

(Clara, 4 October 2020)

I have been meditating for some time to help with my own anxiety issues, so I know the benefits of it. Mindfulness helps me to gain insight on the triggers for my anxiety and also helps me to work on what I need to do to either avoid those triggers or better learn to deal with the things in my life that I cannot change. I think that's an important concept for children to get from mindfulness, knowing that they can use meditation and mindfulness to better control the emotions that threaten responsible decision-making, as well as knowing how to use them to cope with the things they have no control over. I definitely notice that more students are into the meditations that we do each week and honestly, seeing their positive response to the activity does boost my confidence and makes even my teaching of Math better because I feel more of a connection to my students.

(Christina, 10 October 2020)

Another call for teacher preparation programs to recognize the inner lives of teachers comes from Farrell et al. (2020), who make the case for Teaching English to Speakers of Other Languages (TESOL) programs in Canada to move their focus on teaching methods and curricula to the person delivering them. Farrell et al. (2020) propose it should be done "through understanding their spirituality from the perspective of the teacher's personal and professional being and becoming" (p. 338). Anchored on the definition of spirituality as, "a way of being that includes the capacity of humans to see beyond ourselves, to become more than we are, to see mystery and wonder in the world around them, and to experience private and collective moments of awe, wonder, and transcendence" (Schoonmaker, 2009), Farrell (2015) proposes TESOL preparation programs focus on contemplation, helping teachers reach a state of mindfulness or attentiveness in which they can experience an enhanced awareness of thoughts, feeling, emotions, and perceptions.

Farrell (2015) suggests this state of mindfulness can be achieved through techniques such as insight meditation (focusing on the breath, allowing one to focus on what happens each moment as it happens), visualization (visualizing a place or task in which one feels safe, keeping that place or task in mind to help stay calm and relaxed while remaining in a general state of openness), and movement meditation (engaging in yoga, tai-chi, walking, jogging or simple stretching exercises).

150 Tying It All Together

Farrell explains that if tried before teaching, these contemplative practices help teachers gain knowledge of self and become mindful of their attitudes toward their classroom practices and their students' emotions and experiences, as well as promote peacefulness, a clear mind, and a feeling of centeredness.

Contemplative practices can lead to more self-awareness; however, when in contemplation, there is less of a distinction between the contemplator (thinker) and the subject of contemplation (thought). Thus, Farrell (2019) proposes engaging in conscious reflection through reflective practice, in which teachers can consciously think about what they are doing and why they are doing it, such as reflecting on beliefs and classroom practices. He proposes a framework for reflecting on practices that include five stages or levels of reflection: philosophy, principles, theory, practice, and beyond practice.

Philosophy, the first stage, examines the teacher as a person and suggests that professional practice, both inside and outside the classroom, is guided by a teacher's philosophy which has been developed since birth. Thus, teachers are asked to talk or write about their own lives and how they think their past experiences, including their spiritual perspectives and values, may have shaped the construction and development of their basic philosophy of practice.

Principles, the second stage, includes reflection on teachers' assumptions, beliefs (including spiritual beliefs), and conceptions of teaching and learning. Teachers are asked to explore and examine the various images, metaphors, and maxims of teaching and learning (Farrell, 2019; Farrell et al., 2020).

Theory, the third stage of reflection in the proposed framework, considers all aspects of a teacher's planning and the different activities and methods teachers choose as they attempt to put theory into practice. For this stage, teachers describe specific classroom techniques, activities, and routines that they are using or intend to use when carrying out their lessons.

Practice, the fourth stage of reflection, begins with an examination of observable actions while teaching as well as students' reactions or non-reactions during lessons. Teachers can reflect while they are teaching (reflection-in-action), after they teach (reflection-on-action), or before they teach (reflection-for-action). Farrell (2020) explains,

> since teachers do not leave who they are and what they value at the door of their classrooms, but rather tend to interact as whole persons with their whole-person learners, it must be assumed . . . that teachers' spirituality then becomes part of how they conceptualize their professional identities and activities as well as how they attempt to put those conceptions into practice.
>
> *(p. 342)*

The fifth and last stage of reflective practice proposed by Farrell, *Beyond Practice*, entails teachers exploring and examining the moral, political, and social issues

Spirituality as the North Star for Early Childhood Education 151

that impact their practice both inside and outside the classroom. This stage asks teachers to take a more critical reflective stance on their roles and the materials they use, promoting them to become agents of social change who can positively impact learners' lives (T. S. C. Farrell et al., 2020). This stage allows for additional exploring and examining of the impacts of spirituality in interaction with others and with regard to political, social, and moral issues in larger communities and contexts beyond the classroom.

Programs that include reflective practice like the one proposed by Farrell, for TESOL preparation programs, can be extrapolated to all teacher preparation programs and would allow for a move from a focus solely on teaching practices, pedagogy, and curricula, to a focus on the *self who teaches* and how she might have impact upon the students whom she teaches.

Making Spirituality the North Star for Education

Farrell et al. (2020) explain that recent qualitative research within education indicates that teachers' spirituality does in fact help shape their interactions with and applications of disciplinary knowledge (Lindholm & Astin, 2006). As an example of this, the Spirituality in Higher Education project at U.C.L.A.[6] found spirituality to be a major identity factor among professors in the U.S. Eighty-one percent considered themselves to be spiritual 'to some extent' or 'to a great extent,' with 69% also indicating that they look for opportunities for spiritual growth. About 61% reported that they pray or meditate, with or without connections to organized religion. Furthermore, the survey revealed that significant links exist between teacher spirituality and the use of learner-centered, highly effective teaching practices such as small groups and project-based curricula. Lindholm and Astin (2008) concluded that their findings "reinforce the notion that the teaching methods faculty elect to use reflect who they are and what they believe" (p. 198).

Smaller-scale studies also confirm the links between spirituality and teaching. Cecero and Prout (2014), for example, employed a questionnaire that, instead of using faculty ratings of their own spirituality, used students' ratings of faculty spirituality. Their data also revealed significant positive correlations between spirituality and student-centered teaching styles. Other studies suggest the same with specific reference to religious beliefs (Sharma, 2013). From these studies, it can be concluded that spirituality seems to be a potentially significant aspect of teacher identity and practice, and therefore needs to be more explicitly addressed and included within processes of professional reflection and development (Mayes, 2001; Palmer, 2003).

Palmer (2003) explains:

We know we have lost something important in professional training and practice. But we keep looking for it in all the wrong places because the bright light of science has been almost exclusively focused on "objective realities" such as technique, curricula, and cash, rather than on soulful factors such as relational trust. (In fact, we are so obsessed with externals that we will even adopt "objective" measures that weaken relational trust, as high-stakes testing is now doing in too many places.) What does it take to build relational trust? It takes people who are explorers of their own inner lives. It takes people who know something about how to get beyond their own egos; how to withdraw the shadow projections that constantly involve us in making "enemies" out of others; how to forgive and seek forgiveness; how to rejoin soul and role.

(p. 384)

As we move through the COVID-19 pandemic, I believe we are at a potentially pivotal moment in time in which we can revisit what quality education means to us and begin thinking of alternative ways to go back to the essence of early childhood education: to nurture children into uncovering the best possible version of

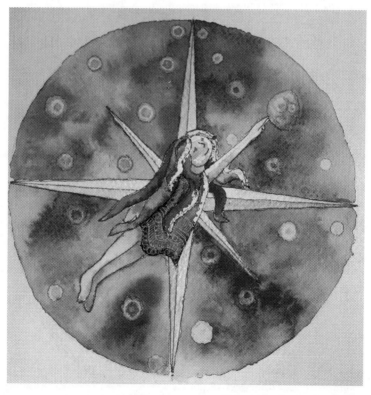

FIGURE 7.1 Spirituality the North Star

Credit: MEG

Spirituality as the North Star for Early Childhood Education **153**

themselves. How do we do it? By nurturing the spirit, being guided and lead by our essence, the soul.

In closing, I want to leave you with an image that, for me, captures what early childhood educators are called to do: free the soul from the confines of the body and the mind and let it express itself to its highest potential. Let's do it. Let's embrace spirituality in education and let it be the North Star that guides us in bringing to fruition our vocation to educate.

Notes

1. For more information on CTT programs in the medical field, visit the Accreditation Council for Graduate Medical Education website www.acgme.org
2. Some of these evaluations can be found on the Center for Courage & Renewal website https://couragerenewal.org/library/longitudinal-evaluation-of-the-courage-to-teach-program/
3. Similarly, to Ms. Escarfuller's experience, shared in Chapter 4, my religious background is Catholic, and as such, I grew up surrounded by the Christian faith and practices. In my case, I was immersed in a culture strongly influenced by Catholicism, based on my country of origin's history. But I struggled with religion for a long time because my beliefs and some of the Catholic practices did not neatly align. I went through a rebellious phase with my faith, and it wasn't until late into my thirties, that I was able to decide on my own, and not because of any societal expectation, to go back to what felt familiar and nurturing to me. Thus, I went back to the Church, and made peace with and embraced being Catholic. Things have changed since then. Now in my late forties, I have distanced myself from the Church again, not because I don't find peace and solace in it, but more so because I do not feel I need religious practices in order to commune with my deepest beliefs. In fact, there are some beliefs I hold dear that would be frowned upon by devout Catholics. These days, I embrace my spirituality, my connections to the spiritual realm, and my strong belief in my own definition of God, without the need of a religious framework to act as a mediator, yet I recognize I will most likely always be culturally Catholic.
4. A few examples of what my students shared as their understanding of spirituality can be found in Chapter 3.
5. Find these resources in my professional website www.drjenmata.com/spirit-lab
6. For more information about this program visit the website for the University of California, Los Angeles, at www.spirituality.ucla.edu

References

Cecero, J. J., & Prout, T. A. (2014). The faculty spirituality questionnaire and its relationship to teaching style. *Religion & Education, 41*, 100–112. https://doi.org/10.1080/15 507394.2014.855084

Center for Courage & Renewal. (2022). *Courage renewal.* Center for Courage & Renewal. Retrieved November 13, 2022, from https://couragerenewal.org/

Farrell, T. S. C. (2015). *Promoting teacher reflection in second language education: A framework for TESOL professionals.* Routledge.

Farrell, T. S. C. (2019). *Reflective practice in ELT.* Equinox Publishing.

Farrell, T. S. C., Baurain, B., & Lewis, M. (2020). 'We teach who we are': Contemplation, reflective practice and spirituality in TESOL. *RELC Journal, 51*(3), 337–346. https://doi.org/10.1177/0033688220915647

Greenfield, C. F. (2018). Investigation into New Zealand early childhood teachers' perspectives on spirituality and Wairua in teaching. *International Journal of Children's Spirituality, 23*(3), 275–290. https://doi.org/10.1080/1364436X.2018.1460333

Lindholm, J. A., & Astin, H. S. (2006). Understanding the 'interior' life of faculty: How important is spirituality? *Religion & Education, 33*, 64–90.

Lindholm, J. A., & Astin, H. S. (2008). Spirituality and pedagogy: Faculty's spirituality and use of student-centered approaches to undergraduate teaching. *Review of Higher Education, 31*, 185–207.

Mata, J. (2012). Nurturing spirituality in early childhood classrooms: The teacher's view. In M. Fowler, J. D. Martin, & J. L. Hochheimer (Eds.), *Spirituality: Theory, praxis and pedagogy* (pp. 239–248). Inter-Disciplinary Press.

Mata, J. (2013a). Meditation: Using it in the classroom. In W. V. Moer, D. A. Celik, & J. L. Hochheimer (Eds.), *Spirituality in the 21st century: Journeys beyond entrenched boundaries* (pp. 109–119). Inter-Disciplinary Press.

Mata, J. (2013b). *Sharing my journey and opening spaces: Spirituality in the classroom global fusion 2013 conference.* Southern Illinois University.

Mata, J. (2015). *Spiritual experiences in early childhood education: Four kindergarteners, one classroom.* Routledge.

Mayes, C. (2001). Cultivating spiritual reflectivity in teachers. *Teacher Education Quarterly, 28*(2), 5–22.

Palmer, P. J. (2003). Teaching with heart and soul: Reflections on spirituality in teacher education. *Journal of Teacher Education, 54*(5), 376–385. https://doi.org/10.1177/0022487103257359

Palmer, P. J. (2007). *The courage to teach: Exploring the inner landscapes of a teacher's life* (10th Anniversary ed.). Jossey-Bass.

Robinson, C. (2019). Young children's spirituality: A focus on engaging with nature. *Australasian Journal of Early Childhood, 44*(4), 339–350. https://doi.org/10.1177/1836939119870907

Schoonmaker, F. (2009). Only those who see take off their shoes: Seeing the classroom as a spiritual space. *Teachers College Record, 111*(12), 2713–2731.

Shange, S. (2019). *Progressive dystopia: Abolition, antiblackness, and schooling in San Francisco.* Duke University Press.

Sharma, B. K. (2013). Hinduism and TESOL: Learning, teaching and student-teacher relationships revisited. *Language and Linguistics Compass, 7*(2), 79–90. https://doi.org/10.1111/lnc3.12013

Souto-Manning, M. (2022). *AERA division K – message from the vice president.* American Educational Research Association (AERA).

Vuorinen, K., Pessi, A. B., & Uusitalo, L. (2021). Nourishing compassion in Finnish kindergarten head teachers: How character strength training influences teacher's other-oriented behavior. *Early Childhood Education Journal, 49*(2), 163–176. https://doi.org/10.1007/s10643-020-01058-0

Waggoner, M. D. (2016). Spirituality and contemporary higher education. *Journal of College and Character, 17*(3), 147–156. https://doi.org/10.1080/2194587X.2016.1195752

INDEX

Note: Page numbers in italics indicate figures. Page numbers followed by "n" indicate a note.

ability to be present, spirituality as 17–19
ability to connect and relate, spirituality as 20–21
Abramson, Lauren 68
abstraction 83; human tendency 83
acceptance, classroom 96–99
Adams, Kate 32
Addition Strip board 84
all of us and more, spirituality as *55*
Alzheimer's 70
American Educational Research Association (AERA), Teacher & Teacher Education 142
AMI Montessori Elementary Guide 69
art 137
Australia 38; children's spirituality in education 59; ethnic identity formation 37
Austria 33
autonomy, of children in school schedule 79
Awakened Brain, The (Miller) 19
awareness, emotional, in classroom 109–112

baby hymn singing (BHS) 29–30
Bank Game 84
behavior management 47–48, 62n1
bell, classroom 97, *98*, 102

Bell Boss 97, 102
Best Self 86
beyond practice, reflection 150–151
Bigger, Stephen 21
bigger than ourselves, spirituality as *56*
Big Questions, Worthy Dreams (Parks) 20
Biology of Belief, The (Lipton) 69, 76
Bloomsbury Handbook of Culture and Identity from Early Childhood to Early Childhood, The 36
body: mind and 31; movement 137; spirituality in *58*
Bone, Jane 20
Bost, Faith 69, 97, 116
Buddhism 67
buffering effect, spirituality as 19

calculation, human tendency 84
Canada 31, 149
Capturing Kids Heart (CKH) training, Flippen Group 102
Carnegie Mellon University 125
Catholic: elementary education 67; faith 66, 67, 153n3; Mass 68
Catholicism 153n3
Cavalletti, Sofia 65
Center for Courage & Renewal website 153n2
Character Clearinghouse (Love) 10

156 Index

children: importance of holistic view 128–130; studies of identity formation 36–39; themes from conversations with 32; values of 31–32
children's spirituality: research on 28–29; studies in education 33–35; studies on meaning-making and relationships to/with God 29–33
Chilean General Law of Education 60
Chödrön, Pema 68
Christ 8
Christian experience, spiritual life 13
classroom: research questions 136–137; teacher role in nurturing spirituality in 130–136; teachers from secular spirituality perspective 136–139
classroom vignettes: bell 97, *98*, 102; Bell Boss 102; connection with nature 117–119; connection with others (friendship) 112–116; contract 94, *95*; emotional awareness 109–112; grace and courtesy lesson 98–99, *99*; gratitude 102–103; gregariousness and conversation 93–94, *95*; hands at work 91, *92*; inner peace 116–117; listening for that inner voice 101–102; material serving child 88, *89*, 90–91; movement revealing 91, 93; openness & acceptance 96–99; peace area 93, *93*; peace rose 97, *100*; preparation as an adult 101; talking piece (Japanese wooden doll) *98*, 103; time and pacing 95–96
Coles, Robert 28
communication, human tendency 85
community, spirituality as *53*
Community Conferencing 68
concentration, human tendency 83–84
Conscious Language course 77, 97, 116
Conscious Parenting Revolution 69, 70, 75, 112
conversation, classroom 93–94, *95*
Courage to Teach (CTT): Palmer's 144, 145–147, 153n1; pedagogical principles and practices 146–147
COVID-19 pandemic 143; ECE seminar 52; inequities and harms in schooling 142; pivotal moment in education 152

CTT *see* Courage to Teach (CTT)
cultural holism 129
curiosity, human tendency 83
curriculum, inclusion of spirituality in 128–130

Denmark, Evangelical Lutheran Church 29
depression, spirituality as buffering effect 19
Divine 8
Dominican Republic 68
dreams, spiritual development 138–139
Dr. Jekyll and Dr. Hyde, identity 64

early childhood education (ECE): capstone internship seminar on 130; profession of 128–129; redesigned seminar 147, 148
Early Childhood Educators' Spiritual Practices in the Classroom (ECE-SPC) 139–140n2
ECE *see* early childhood education (ECE)
education: inequities in 142–143; making spirituality the North Star 151–153; studies on children's spirituality in 33–35
educators: research on, perception on spirituality 49–61; *see also* teacher(s)
Einstein, Albert 65
Elkins, David 13
emotional awareness, classroom 109–112
emotional wheel 118, *119*
Energy Codes Coach 101
England: children's identity 36; conversations with children 32
environment, connection with nature 117–119
Escarfuller, Ms. 61, 72; *see also* classroom vignettes
establishment clause, U.S. Constitution 127
Evangelical Lutheran Church, Denmark 29
exactness, human tendency 84
exploration, human tendency 82

fairness, children's values 32
Fairy World, projective method 39
feedback loop 73, 103
finding meaning, Montessori great lesson 103–108

Index 157

First Amendment, U.S. Constitution 2, 127
Fisher 16-item Feeling Good, Living Life 33
Flippen Group, Capturing Kids Heart (CKH) training 102
flowering paradox, spring metaphor 146
Foster, Carla 72, 79
Fowler, James 20
Frady, Kathy 30
free exercise clause, U.S. Constitution 127
Freire, Paolo 126
friendship, connection with others 112–116

Geometric Cabinet: child work *89*; material serving child 88, 90–91
George Washington Carver DISCO STEAM Inverturers 118
God 8, 10, 32; categories of 104; creator above us *106*; creator among us *106*; on the cross *109*; as judge *108*; as nature *107*; as protector from evil *104*; as protector with hug *105*; as provider *108*; studies on children's relationships to/with 29–33; understanding of 125–126
Godly Play, grounded theory approach 30
Goodliff, Gill 36
Grace & Courtesy lesson, classroom 98–99, *99*
Gracie, Anita 134, 135
gratitude, classroom 102–103
Great Lesson: Coming of the Universe 103–105, 107–108; Montessori 103–108
Greenfield, Cheryl Faye 57–58
gregariousness: classroom 93–94, *95*; human tendency 85

hands at work 91, *92*; classroom 91, *92*
happiness, spirituality as *54*
Harris, Kathleen 36, 138
Hart, Tobin 51
Haslip, Michael 52
Hay, David 28
Heart and Soul, Palmer 144
higher education, supporting children's spirituality starting in 143–144
Highest Self 65, 66, 67, 68, 70, 77, 78, 82, 86
holism and the soul 129
Holistic Curriculum, The (Miller) 129

holistic education: cultural holism 129; holism and the soul 129; natural holism 128–129
holistic view of development, spirituality as 16–17
Hong Kong, Waldorf school in 55
human nature, spirituality as *15*
human potential, spirituality as innate 17–19
Human Tendencies and Montessori Education, The (Montessori) 81–82
Hyde, Brendan 20, 38

identity: Jekyll and Hyde 64; studies on formation of children's 36–39
imagination, human tendency 84
imitation, human tendency 83
Indonesia 37
Industrial Revolution 127
innate human potential, spirituality as 17–19
inner guide 9
inner peace, classroom 116–117
insight meditation 149
International Handbook of Holistic Education 128, 129
interpretive phenomenological analysis (IAP) method 60

Jenkins, Peggy 77
Jesus 32; Jesus and children (Mark 10:13–16) 30
John Templeton Foundation 23n1
justice, children's values 32

karakia 59, 62n6
Kibble, David 17
kindergarten classrooms, children's spirituality in 33–35
Krishnamurti, Jiddu 113
Kuttner, Fred 69

Laws of the Universe 65
life's meaning and purpose, spirituality to rediscover 21–23
Lipton, Bruce 69, 76
listening for that inner voice, classroom 101–102
Love, Patrick 10–11
Lovelock, Pauline 32

Margaritis, Sister 66–68
Mark 10:13–16, Jesus and children 30

158 Index

Mata, Dr. J 86, 110
materialism 40n4
meaning-making, studies on children's
spiritual 29–33
meditation 35, 138
Miller, John P. 129
Miller, Lisa 19
Miller, Ron 129
mindfulness 149, 149–150
Montessori, Maria 66, 74, 78, 84, 85,
103, 112, 117; self-perfection and
self-awareness 72; sopranatura or
supernature 81
Montessori, Mario M. 81–86
Montessori great lessons, story of coming
of the universe 103–108
Montessori Primary, Geometric Cabinet
74, 88, 90–91
moral compass 9
movement: classroom 91, 93; human
tendency 82; movement
meditation 149
MRI (magnetic resonance imaging) 19
Multidimensional Measure of
Religiousness/Spirituality (MRS)
37
Multigroup Ethnic Identity Measure
(MEIM) 37
music 137

National Association for the Education
of Young Children (NAEYC),
Developmentally Appropriate
Practices (DAP) 128–129, 136
National Curriculum Council, England's
21
National Tulip Citizen Project 118
natural holism 128–129
nature: connection with 117–119;
spirituality incorporating 138;
spirituality in relation to 57
negative-positive dimension, religiousness
and spirituality 8
New Age concepts 8
New Zealand 56–57, 138
1946 London Lectures, The (Montessori) 85
Non-Violent Communication (NVC) 68,
75, 111, 112
North Star 3, 123, 142, 143; making
spirituality, for education 151–153;
spirituality as *152*
Norway 30

*Nurturing Spirituality in Children in
the Non-Sectarian Classroom*
(Jenkins) 77
Nutcracker Ballet 68
Nye, Rebecca 28

observation, human tendency 83
openness, classroom 96–99
order, human tendency 83
organized-person dimension, religiousness
and spirituality 8
organized religion 8
orientation, human tendency 83
orientation association area (OAA) 18
Original Vision, The (Robinson) 40n3
otherness, spirituality as *15*, 51

Palmer, Parker 20, 128; Courage to Teach
(CTT) 144, 145–147; "flowering
paradox" metaphor 146; Heart and
Soul 144
Parks, Sharon 20
peace area, classroom 93, *93*
peace rose, classroom 97, *100*
pedagogy, Montessori human tendencies
and 81–86
pedagogy, spirituality informing 69–81;
'full, complete, and equal' 78–79;
'it's all in our favor' 74–75; 'needs,
mattering, and growth' 79–81;
perfection 69–74; purpose 74;
we are spiritual beings, energy,
and manifesters 76–78; *see also*
spirituality
pedagogy of the soul, Palmer 145
philosophy, reflection 150
physicalism 40n4
Positive Discipline 47
positivity, spirituality as *54*
practice, reflection 150
preparation as adult, classroom 101
principles, reflection 150
Progressive Dystopia (Shange) 142

Quaker way of life 68
Quantum Enigma, The (Rosenblum and
Kuttner) 69

Rahim, Akil 118
reflection: beyond practice 150–151;
philosophy 150; practice 150;
principles 150; theory 150

religion: components of 9; definition 2, 10; organized 8; spirituality *vs* 12

Religions, Values and Peak-Experiences (Maslow) 40n3

religiosity, differentiating spirituality from 10–12

Religious Education (RE) classroom 134

religious enculturation 30

religiousness and spirituality, constructs 8

religious practices 7

repetition, human tendency 84

Representation Project 95

research questions, in-service childhood educators 136–137

Robinson, Christine 59

Rosenberg, Marshall B. 68, 75, 111, 112

Rosenblum, Bruce 69

safe spaces, children's spiritual development 33–34

SBNR (spiritual but not religious) 11

Scandinavia 30

Schein, Deborah 52

Search Institute 17, 23n1

Second Vatican Council 13

Secret Spiritual World of Children, The (Hart) 51

secularism 8

secular spirituality 14

Self 20, 129; *see also* Highest Self; Soulful Self

self-control, human tendency 85

self-perfection, human tendency 84

sense of self, spirituality and 36–39

SEP *see* spiritual education program (SEP)

separation of church and state 2, 127–128

September 11, 2001 1

sewing, hands at work 91, *92*

Shange, Savannah 142

Singer, Hui-Ling 101

Soulful Self 65

South Africa 32, 33; themes from conceptions of spirituality 32–33

Souto-Manning, Marianna 142–143

SPECT (single-photon emission computed tomography) 18

Spirit 65

Spiritual Child, The (Hay and Nye) 28

spiritual education program (SEP) 35

Spiritual Experiences in Early Childhood Education (Mata-McMahon) 28

spirituality: ability to be present 17–19; ability to connect and relate 20–21; children's 1–2; concept of 7; defining 12–23, 64–69; definition by categories *15*; definition of 2, 7, 149; differentiating from religiosity 10–12; as holistic view of development 16–17; inclusion in classroom 128–130; as innate human potential 17–19; making, the North Star for education 151–153; moral compass 9; rediscovering life's meaning and purpose 21–23; religion *vs 12*; religiousness and 8; research on educators' perception 49–61; scholars defining 14–15; secular 14; supporting children's, in higher education 143–144; *see also* pedagogy, spirituality informing

Spirituality in Higher Education project, U.C.L.A. 151

Spiritual Lives of Children, The (Coles) 28

Sputnik 127

Stages of Faith, The (Fowler) 20

Stamp Game 79, 84

Statistics and Machine Learning 125

St Francis of Assisi School, New Orleans 66

storytelling 137; Montessori classroom 80–81

substantial-functional dimension, religiousness and spirituality 8

Sweden 31

talking piece, classroom *98*, 103

teacher(s): candidates 131, 132; in-service 135; preparation programs 3; pre-service 134, 137–138; pre-service student 131, 133; role in nurturing spirituality in classroom 130–136; secular spirituality perspective of 136–139

Teaching English to Speakers of Other Languages (TESOL) programs 151; Canada 149

Ted Talks 112

tendencies, human 81–86

TESOL *see* Teaching English to Speakers of Other Languages (TESOL) programs

160 Index

Te Whāriki Curriculum, New Zealand 56–59, 139
theory, reflection 150
Thich Nhat Hanh 68
time and pacing, classroom 95–96
To Educate the Human Potential (Montessori) 72
tragic expressions 75
Transcending the Talented Tenth (James) 40n3
Trousdale, Ann 20
Tulip Project 118; work *120*

unifying with "something other", spirituality as *15*
University of California, Los Angeles (U.C.L.A.) 151, 153n6
University of Minnesota 68
U.S. Constitution: establishment clause 127; First Amendment 2, 127; free exercise clause 127; separation of church and state 2, 127–128; understanding constraints 126–128
U.S. Department of Education 120n1

visualization 149

wairua 57–59, 62n4, 139
Walach, Harald16
whakapapa 59, 62n7
Wilkinson, Jacqueline 134, 135
Winter-Sellery, Katherine 69, 70, 73, 75, 77, 112, 113, 115, 116
work/activity, human tendency 84

yoga 138, 149
YouTube 112

Zhang, Kaili Chen 55

Printed in the United States
by Baker & Taylor Publisher Services